THE GRAMMAR OF OUR CIVILITY

THE GRAMMAR OF OUR CIVILITY

CLASSICAL EDUCATION IN AMERICA

Lee T. Pearcy

Baylor University Press
Waco, Texas 76798

Book Design by Diane Smith
Cover Design by Cynthia Dunne

Add any permissions for cover art, article reproduction, etc. [use statements
provided by the supplier of the art or article when possible]

Library of Congress Cataloging-in-Publication Data

Pearcy, Lee T., 1947-
The grammar of our civility : classical education in America / Lee T. Pearcy.
p. cm.
Includes bibliographical references and index.
ISBN 1-932792-16-3 (pbk. : alk. paper)
1. Classical education. 2. Education--United States. I. Title.

LC1011.P43 2005
480'.71'073--dc22

2005004101

Printed in the United States of America on acid-free paper

For
William M. Calder III

te sequor, o Graiae gentis decus, inque tuis nunc
ficta pedum pono pressis vestigia signis

Lucr. *DRN* 3.3–4

CONTENTS

FOREWORD

This short book has been a long time in the making, although the actual writing of it occupied me for only five years, from 1999 until the summer of 2004. Its genesis, though, can be traced to the autumn of 1984, when I found myself enmeshed very much against my will in a power struggle of the kind that too often disfigures academic life at the University of Texas and elsewhere.[1] During the rest of that long academic year in Austin, I sat down nearly every morning with my friend Carl Rubino to discuss the situation before us. Our conversation turned again and again to an old, difficult question: what was the connection between knowledge and action? Specifically, what was the connection between knowledge of classical literature and culture, which we agreed was profound and beautiful, and moral action in society? This book is an attempt to answer that question.

My answer takes its departure from a remark of Werner Jaeger: "Without the continuing prestige of the ancient idea of humanity in human culture, classical scholarship is just a waste of time. Whoever does not see this ought to come to America and let himself learn from

---

[1] Briefly described by Robert Gutzwiller in Culham and Edmunds, *Classics: A Discipline and Profession in Crisis?* 355–57.

the way classical studies have developed there."[2] I argue that Jaeger was right. Classics, the study of ancient Greece and Rome, has never developed, as other academic subjects and disciplines have, a distinctly American form in response to American social and cultural conditions. Instead, Classics in this country has imitated European models and patterned itself after forms of education and scholarship developed in a cultural context where, as Jaeger saw, the prestige of Humanism guaranteed the cultural value of classical study.

This American dependence on European models of classical education followed naturally from the place that study of Greece and Rome had in American higher education from its beginning. Because classical languages formed the ground of higher and secondary education in America from Colonial times, classics could hardly be seen in anything but traditional terms and so was unable to negotiate successfully the transition at the end of the nineteenth century from what Gerald Graff and others have called the Old College to the modern university. Classics retained much of its predisciplinary, untheorized character and as a result became, and continues to become, marginalized among the professionalized disciplines of modern American universities. Finally, I imagine the contours of a distinctive form of classical education grounded in American personal and social reality as firmly as European classical studies were grounded in the society they served.

In writing about this predisciplinary, untheorized academic practice, I have tried to resist the temptation to beg questions by offering a unitary definition that would limit my investigation to the answers that I hoped to find. I speak therefore sometimes about Classics (a singular noun), sometimes about classical studies or classical education, and sometimes by metynomy about Latin, Greek, or classical languages. I find this imprecision unsatisfying but necessary, and I hope to clarify it in a more theoretical work whose outlines are only now beginning to emerge.

This book is not only for classical scholars, a few thousand of whom still practice their craft in America; indeed, much of what it says will not

[2]   Jaeger, *Scripta Minora*, vol. 1, xxvi.

be news to them. Instead I have written for the body of educated Americans who may have some vague recollection of high school Latin, or of a college humanities course, and who may believe, without knowing exactly why, that there is something important about the cultures of ancient Greece and Rome and the languages that convey them.

I am conscious that after twenty years away from university life, I write now as someone for whom it has become almost a foreign country, albeit one that I visit regularly. I hope, however, that this point of view has allowed me to notice and comment on things that those who live there take for granted, and that my comments will be taken not as those of an alien, but as those of an expatriate.

No one writes alone. It is a pleasure here to thank a few of the people who helped in the creation of this book. My two academic homes, The Episcopal Academy and Bryn Mawr College, have given me students to teach and room to work and think, and the librarians at Bryn Mawr's Carpenter and Canaday Libraries have never failed to produce the materials that support my investigations. Kathryn Pearcy never failed to support me in other ways. Barbara Gold lent her example as I thought about Classics as a part of American culture. Ward Briggs, Judith Hallett, and Alexander Pearson read, commented on, and improved early drafts of parts of the book. Martha Gimbel helped me verify references, and our shared reading of the *Iliad* during the academic year 2003–2004 led me to make important changes in Chapter 4. Carey Newman was (and is) the best and most scholarly of editors, and his suggestions have made this a better, more readable book.

Conversations with many people have helped me think about classical education. Many are not classicists, and some may be unaware of what project our conversations were aiding. None bears any responsibility for my obstinate persistence in error. All have my gratitude: Henry Bender, Deena Berg, Rebecca Bushnell, Jay Crawford, Robert Cronin, Joseph Farrell, Mary French, Julia Gaisser, Richard Hamilton, Jane Wilson Joyce, Michael Klaassen, William Levitan, the late Frank McAlpin, Kathryn Mulvihill, Sheila Murnaghan, the late Gareth Morgan, Gregory Nagy, James O'Donnell, Douglass Parker, the late John Plant, John Powell, Ralph Rosen, Matthew Santirocco, The Rev. James Squire, Richard Thomas, and Larisa Warhol. Among my teachers now deceased let me mention particularly Steele Commager, Moses Hadas, Gilbert Highet, and Agnes Kirsopp Lake Michels. Finally, the dedication acknowledges a professional friendship that began forty years ago when William M. Calder III began to inspire me, as he has inspired many others, to think about classical scholarship and its history.

Stoddartsville
August 15, 2004

Chapter 1

THE GRAMMAR OF OUR CIVILITY

I want to talk about what happens when language no longer describes things, when words slip their moorings in reality. I want to make the case for paying attention to a form of education that hardly anyone in American universities practices.

Here is what happened.

Coca-Cola. Aspirin. Yellow boxes of dynamite. Bulldozers. Nails. Cartons of Luckies. Two-way radios. Diesel fuel. Hand grenades. Eveready batteries. Iodine. Flour. Artillery shells.

The soldiers came suddenly, bringing all these things and more. The islanders watched airstrips unroll in the jungle, C-47's bumble down, more and more things move down the ramps. The white men's world and its war made no sense to the islanders. They knew only that the foreign soldiers called their wealth "cargo," and that when certain things were done, Cargo came.

Then the soldiers were gone.

The islanders tried to bring back the strangers and their wealth. They built landing strips in the jungle, control towers of logs lashed together, radios of twigs with dials made of stone and seashells. They performed the rites of summoning Cargo as they had seen the visitors perform them.

No Cargo came. The islanders were not discouraged. Cargo had come, once upon a time; there was no doubt of it. If it did not come now, the problem was with their performance of the rites or with their faith. They constructed, gradually, an elaborate system to make sense of every particular of what they were doing, including its internal contradictions. In this system they found consolation and meaning.

In modern American universities professors of Classics, the study of ancient Greece and Rome, continue to perform rites that once worked. They teach and study Greek and Latin literature, sift what evidence there is for the history of Greece and Rome, pore over manuscripts, and examine sherds. Few of them, once beyond the first steps in their profession, give much thought to why they do these things. They enjoy what they do, they are good at it, and there is a living to be made. If someone asks what good these activities do (a slightly different and harder question), the professors may hesitate, but sooner or later they answer, and their answers always contain the same theme. The professors appeal for validation of their activities to known and verifiable historical circumstances. Classics, they suggest, is an important subject and worth doing because it has nearly always been important and worth doing. From roughly the Renaissance to the First World War, Classics was at the center of a certain kind of European and American education. To be educated, to be civilized, to be a gentleman, meant to be acquainted with the languages, literature, and culture of ancient Greece and Rome.

The professors are right. Education in the vanished cultures of Greece and Rome once formed an intelligible system of theory, technique, and practice. The system was essential and was seen to be essential within the societies it served. It was a code, but the code made sense because it expressed a single, if manifold, purpose. In all societies where it dominated education in the Renaissance and after, Classics was designed to form the tastes, values, and attitudes of the governing class.

The great beings did appear with their Cargo, once upon a time not so long ago, when every schoolboy knew his Latin and some knew their Greek. But what classicists do now must seem to an external observer as absurd as trying to summon a C-47 full of chocolate bars with a radio made of palm fronds and seashells.

University teaching, in any subject, is full of absurdities. The researcher at the edge of knowledge must teach the undergraduate needing remedial work. Two faculty members in the same field may have hardly any point of intellectual contact, so that a man beavering away on "IG II236: The So-called Foundation Charter of the Corinthian League—a Heresy?" may have nothing whatever to discuss with a woman thinking hard on her next paper, "*Grenouilles de Passage*: Aristophanes' Liminal Frogs."[1]

It is not, however, the contradictions shared with other fields that make Classics resemble an intellectual Cargo Cult. The contrast between how university teachers of Classics think about their field and how they present it in the classroom, or between one researcher's jargon and another's, does not account for the peculiar existential dilemma of Classics. That absurdity comes from the contrast between vanished Cargo and twigs and stones, between the sophistication, coherence, and directed purpose of traditional classical education and the naïve, fragmented, aimless parody that passes for Classics in most universities today.

Well-meaning people sometimes speak of education as a set of messages to be transmitted from teacher to student. When a student can recall or repeat the message, when the student knows who wrote *Don Quixote* or what were the three principal causes of the Vietnam War, education has taken place. Multiple-choice tests can measure the transmission, and numbers can express its efficiency.

If the analogy with transmitting a message contributes to an accurate description of education, then we have no choice but to conclude that many of the best and most creative minds have been those for whom education has failed. They persist, and we hope they persist, in getting the messages wrong. Einstein, a story goes, refused to memorize his telephone number or any other fact that he could look up. The tale may be apocryphal.[2] It is suspiciously close to the cliché of the absent-minded professor and to the late Romantic notion that the creative mind is unfettered by trivialities. Sherlock Holmes, readers of the Canon will recall, refused to clutter his mind with irrelevant facts like the Copernican system.[3] Einstein, absent-minded professor, and fictional consulting detective embody a widely held conviction: the best minds are those for whom any message they have received from education is far less important than the new meanings into which they transform what they have learned. Even for the person who is not an Einstein, or a professor at all, education works best when it equips him to create new messages for new contexts.

A better analogy comes to mind. Education is not a message but the grammar of a language called culture. This grammar is not transmitted; it is acquired. Whoever acquires it is free from the limitations imposed by the facts he has learned. Just as someone who knows a language can generate sentences that he has never been taught, so someone who has been educated can generate new ideas, new interpretations of old facts, new statements about reality. The great, creative intellects are those for whom education as grammar has not failed. They are those who have mastered the language which that grammar describes and makes possible.

Everyone who has learned to speak another language has had the joyous experience of moving from simple parroting of phrases in context to creating sentences in contexts, from uttering the noise that means "Good morning" to being able to say whether it is or might be a good or bad morning, a good morning or a good car. Grammar is the code that enables us to make that move and others of greater complexity. By coming to an explicit or intuitive understanding of a language's grammar, we become able to apply the facts of language to reality. We may learn a new way of thinking—or even of dreaming.[4]

Education also, to the extent that it resembles acquiring a language rather than using a phrase book, depends on a grammar of culture. Sometimes (more often than not, nowadays) the grammars in education are implicit and unexpressed, and those who use them are unaware that they exist. But many people speak a language well without any explicit awareness of the code that enables them to do so. Sometimes education is more or less explicitly grammatical, although the grammars may be a very poor description of the cultures of teachers and learners. And sometimes societies manage to create a form of education that encodes the babble of culture into a system that rationalizes and explains the culture's contradictions and makes possible the orderly, sensible creation of new forms and statements within that culture. Such a grammar makes it easier to educate and easier to acquire an education.

Between the Renaissance and the First World War the governing classes in Britain and America came to the richness of Western high culture through an artificial structure whose purposes were to explain that civilization and ease the way to its complexities and hard truths, and to encode values and attitudes that tempered and strengthened the collective self-awareness of those classes. That artificial structure or enabling code, that grammar of civility, was classical education.

The analogy between education in a culture and the grammar of a language is profound and fertile. It makes it possible to be more precise about the sense in which the activities of university teachers of Classics resemble the Cargo Cult of Pacific Islanders. Those innocent, insular people failed to notice that the success of certain activities in their culture during a certain period in history depended on circumstances of which they had no inkling and causes over which they could have no control. They clung to what they could understand and continued as best they could the activities that had, under those special circumstances, brought success. They created a kind of false grammar, a system that made sense on its own terms but preserved only the external appearance of what had once been reality. They tried to make radios of twigs, shells, and feathers.

The natives of university departments of Classics have failed to notice the disappearance of the language whose grammar was their practice. The culture of the governing class that classical education once served has disappeared. The fact of a governing class, of course, has not, but the executives, bureaucrats, managers, and legislators of modern America share no single, coherent, humane culture. Decision makers often seem to lack any awareness that they form a governing class.

Their failure to acknowledge what they are may be not so much duplicity as genuine ignorance. They are not seeking to conceal their working as an elite in democratic or nominally democratic societies; rather, they have simply never been educated to an awareness of their role. Those who might have helped them understand have forgotten that they once knew how to do so.

The professors have also forgotten *why* Classics was once important. In ignorance of their new circumstances, they have created a false grammar. Their practice of their profession makes sense on its own terms, but it is connected only weakly to the society and culture within which they act. Teaching Classics in a university appears increasingly to be a marginal activity or an irrelevant curiosity. Artificial intelligence, evolutionary biology, cosmology, and other academic subjects that have the potential to make true and powerful statements about our culture are far removed from classical studies. The excitement is elsewhere. The great beings who once were here have moved on.

In creating their false grammar, the professors have had to create false paradigms. In the classical languages, traditional grammar creates paradigms, patterns according to which the forms of words can be generated. Generations of children learn to chant the declension of *mensa* or conjugate *amo*, *amas*, *amat*. Like the grammars of Greek and Latin, classical education can be seen as a series of paradigms. The description, and the analogy, can be made to go further. The lesser paradigms group themselves into systems, and two systems dominate the others. As classical ideas about grammar tend to organize language into words for things—nouns—and words for actions—verbs—so classical education has been organized around two fundamental ways of thinking about the aims and methods of education. One way of thinking emphasizes things, the objective, scholarly study of what survives from classical antiquity. For that mode of thinking about classical education I shall use a German term, *Altertumswissenschaft*. The term is not as cumbersome as it may seem. Why I have chosen to use it and what exactly it means will become clear shortly. The second way of thinking about classical education emphasizes not things but processes. It is concerned less with the remains of antiquity in themselves than with their effect on those in the present who are exposed to them. This second way of thinking about classical education had, from its origins, a familiar name: liberal arts education.

Together, liberal arts education and *Altertumswissenschaft* formed the grammar of classical education.[5] Until early in this century, that grammar reflected a language in which meaningful statements could be made: the culture and attitudes of the European and American governing classes. From, very roughly, the Renaissance until the First World War, classical education made sense because of the interaction in it of these two paradigmatic beliefs. During this period, any belief that was paradigmatic for classical education was also paradigmatic for Western high culture. Amid the ruins of that culture, its broken phrases and fragments of utterance are admired and only half understood by the new Goths and Vandals, the managers and professional persons, encamped among them. Now let us rehearse the true paradigms. Then let us examine those quaint people, the professors of Classics, and the false paradigms they have created to make sense of their new world and their new masters.

LIBERAL ARTS

The first true paradigm is liberal arts education.

Commencement speakers at liberal arts colleges are fond of invoking the medieval canon of the Seven Liberal Arts and the ancient idea of liberal arts as the skills appropriate to a free citizen. In doing so they are giving liberal arts education a pedigree longer than it deserves.[6] Like so many other things, it began in the Renaissance and was given its full modern form only in the nineteenth century. If liberal arts education is to be traced to any single time and place, it is not to antiquity or the Middle Ages but to the Renaissance and to the career of humanists like Vittorino da Feltre.[7]

In 1428 Vittorino came to Mantua at the invitation of Gianfresco Gonzaga, the local ruler, to educate the Gonzaga children. Vittorino's program sounds simple and familiar to anyone acquainted with early

twentieth-century Andover, Exeter, or Saint Paul's. In the early fif-
teenth century, his educational practice was revolutionary. Vittorino's
students were to board with him, and he was to look after their moral
and spiritual education as well as their intellectual development. The
curriculum consisted of roughly equal amounts of exercise and games,[8]
Christianity, and study of Greek and Latin Classics. Each student was
to be treated as an individual, and the work tailored to his or her—
Gianfresco had daughters—abilities. A few promising middle-class students were admitted and treated on exactly the same terms as the
Gonzaga children and those of the other first families of Milan.

Vittorino did not intend his school to produce Latin secretaries,
bureaucrats, or clergymen. His aim was Platonist and, as we would see
it, elitist. He wanted to educate the guardians; that is, to take those who
would in any case rule and those who might be admitted to the governing class and to form their minds and souls in such a way that they
would be the best rulers. Vittorino's pupils studied Latin and Greek not
because they would need them in their jobs—a prince, after all, does not
have a job—but because classical languages, literature, history, and art
provided the best paradigms for the thought and conduct of a governing class.

The subject we call Classics and the kind of education we call liberal arts began in the Renaissance and are the creation of men like
Vittorino da Feltre. From their common beginning, in fact, Classics and
liberal arts were indistinguishable. This classical or liberal education
needs to be distinguished from the practical, vocational education in
Latin, logic, and rhetoric offered in the medieval and later universities.
People who complain about the modern university's emphasis on professional education would do well to remember that they cannot base
their complaints on history. Universities were professional schools from
their medieval beginning, designed, as a fifteenth-century Oxford document put it, for "encrese of clergy and konnyng men; to the goode gov-
ernaunce and prosperitie of the Reme of Englond withoute end."[9] The
medieval universities taught Latin grammar and rhetoric, logic (by way
of Aristotle in Latin translation), law, medicine, and theology, all prac-

tical and professional subjects. These subjects were taught in Latin and based on Aristotle, Pliny, Galen, and other ancient authors, but their Latin and antiquity do not make them classical. They lack the explicit dependence of Renaissance humanists on the ethical and moral power that they found in ancient Greece and Rome, and they lack the frank elitism of Classics, in the Renaissance and after. "The older system," one recent analysis states, "had fitted perfectly the needs of the Europe of the high middle ages, with its communes, its church offices open to the low-born of high talents and its vigorous debates on power and authority in state and church. The new system . . . fitted the needs of the new Europe that was taking shape, with its closed governing elites, hereditary offices and strenuous efforts to close off debate on vital political and social issues."[10]

Renaissance classical education—humanistic, Christian, and designed to educate members of the governing class by exposing them to the best patterns of conduct, modes of thinking, and products of culture, rather than to train bureaucrats and clerics in Latin, logic, and rhetoric—gained a firm hold on education in the English-speaking world in the seventeenth and eighteenth centuries. Its domination of the elite secondary schools like Eton and Winchester was complete. In the universities, the new learning replaced the Aristotelian, scholastic curriculum of the medieval *studium generale*; and fee-paying, aristocratic and upper-middle-class students, future courtiers, bishops, rural magnates and country squires, filled the colleges in place of the medieval university's poor clerks.[11]

With its success, humanistic classical education had its critics, and not only from the ranks of those put off by its elitism and inevitable connection with the governing class it was designed to form. In seventeenth-century Oxford, John Locke, who knew the classical curriculum from the inside as a tutor of Greek and rhetoric at Christ Church, found it wanting. "Can there be anything more ridiculous," he asked, "than that a father should waste his own money, and his son's time, in setting him to learn the Roman language? . . . Could it be believed, unless we have every where amongst us examples of it, that a child should be forced to learn the rudiments of a language, which he is never to use in the course of life that he is designed to, and neglect all the while the writing a good hand, and casting accounts, which are of great advantage in all conditions of life, and to most trades indispensably necessary?"[12]

Locke's criticisms struck at a vulnerable point in classical education. As a tool for shaping the ethics and culture of the upper ranks of society, Classics was rigorous and effective, "absolutely necessary for a gentleman," as Locke said. As an instrument of general education applied to the middle classes, it was soft and useless. But merchants, parish clergy, and physicians will want their children to have the same education as noblemen, bishops, and gentlemen scientists. It is natural to look upon the education of society's best as society's best education and to want that education for the children one hopes will become part of the governing class. Thus Classics spread, inevitably and rapidly, to grammar schools and obscure private academies.[13] English universities, although they became increasingly preserves of the upper and upper middle classes in the seventeenth and eighteenth centuries, never entirely lost their tradition of admitting poor students. The universities' curricula were never exclusively classical, but to anyone who hoped to use his wits to gain access to power and privilege, Classics and the university education to which they led were the best road.

During the nineteenth century the monopoly of Classics was threatened. Locke's fundamental criticism of classical education, that it was impractical, gained force from new developments in science and technology. It was no longer a matter of classically educated businessmen who were ignorant of "writing a good hand, and casting accounts." There were large areas of knowledge that had a claim on the attention of educated people, and these areas were not in the classical education invented by Vittorino da Feltre and the humanists of the Renaissance. Many mid-Victorians might have shared Charles Darwin's verdict on his classical education: "Nothing could have been worse for the development of my mind."[14]

The attack on Classics came from two directions. One was Locke's: an education based on Greek and Latin was useless in the modern world, and there were practical subjects that ordinary people would do better to study. The other attack was more subtle and struck at the connection between Classics and the governing classes. Not only, this second line of attack went, was Classics useless for most people; its traditional function, shaping the intellectual culture and ethical standards of the governing classes, could be done as well or better by other subjects. Science in the modern nineteenth century, or modern languages and history, could do the job as well as Classics had in the Renaissance.

No serious person would now dispute this proposition, but in the nineteenth century the utilitarian attack on classical education produced a serious defender and a redefinition of the Renaissance idea of shaping character through study of Greece and Rome. Oddly enough, the new idea was to have a more profound effect on undergraduate education in America than in Britain, where it originated. As early as 1866, John Henry Newman was being quoted by university reformers in the United States.[15]

NEWMAN'S CLASSICAL UNIVERSITY

In the spring of 1851 the archbishop of Armagh wrote to John Henry Newman asking for Newman's help in founding a university for Roman Catholics in Ireland. Newman was a recent convert to Catholicism, but education, as he wrote in his journal some years later, was his line from first to last. From 1822 until his conversion in 1845 he was a fellow of Oriel College, Oxford. There he had been one of the founders of the Tractarian movement, which sought to return the Church of England to the apostolic theology and liturgical worship from which the Tractarians felt it had departed. Newman the educationist remembered that Tractarianism began in a dispute among the dons at Oriel over the proper role of a college tutor: was he to teach only a subject and syllabus, or did he have a pastoral role as well and some responsibility for his pupils' ethical development and spiritual welfare? Newman argued strongly for the pastoral idea of teaching.

In 1852 Newman, chosen as the first rector of the new Catholic University of Ireland, delivered a series of lectures in Dublin setting out the basic principles on which he believed a university should be founded. The considerably revised published version of the Dublin lectures is what people mean when they speak of Newman's *Idea of a University*. Together with Newman's numerous other essays and addresses on university subjects, they make up a coherent body of thought and analysis, the product of a lifetime spent thinking seriously about what education is for.[16]

Newman's answer is that university education is not *for* anything at all. A university, he says, is a place of teaching universal knowledge, and knowledge has no other goal than itself. The purpose of a university education is to develop the intellect and to produce a person who can learn anything whatever. A university will, of course, do other things as well. People who fasten onto Newman's idea of knowledge for its own sake often fail to notice that his ideal university has a place for practical and professional subjects, just as they often ignore the religious motivation behind his attempt to define a university. But education for a profession, education for research, and education for God are not the essence of Newman's university. "If its object," he says, "were scientific and philosophical discovery, I do not see why a University should have students; if religious training, I do not see how it can be the seat of literature and science."[17]

Newman articulated the modern idea of liberal arts education, beloved of commencement speakers, honored in the curricula of places as different as Columbia University in New York and Carleton College in Northfield, Minnesota, and given a certain amount of lip service even at universities whose main emphasis is petroleum engineering or agricultural management. He provided the forms, and in some cases the words, that advocates of liberal education in the twentieth century have used to defend their position against the attacks of Locke and his intellectual descendants. Yet Newman was a conservative so profound that his thought stands apart from nearly every important nineteenth-century intellectual movement, especially Marxism and Darwinism.[18]

Here, in the influence of Newman's ideas on the modern understanding of liberal arts, lies one reason for the importance of Classics in education. Newman's liberal arts are Classics—a point often overlooked by those who invoke Newman without reading him and imagine that liberal arts means "general education" or "some subjects that aren't scientific, mathematical, or professional."

Newman does not say in so many words that by liberal arts education he means education based on the study of Latin and Greek and of classical literature. In 1852 he would not have had to. Most of his audience knew no other kind of secondary or undergraduate education and would have understood that by "liberal studies," "liberal arts," or "liberal education" he meant very nearly what we would mean by Classics; in the same way, his audience would have known that when he specified "Grammar" and "Metrical Composition" among the subjects a boy should study, he meant the grammar of the classical languages and verse composition in Latin and Greek. In any case, his aim in the lectures of 1852 was to set out an attitude toward university education and to define its aims and purposes, not to specify the subjects that a university education ought to include.[19]

In one of his supplements to *The Idea of a University*, Newman is more specific. The essay called "Christianity and Letters" takes up a central point of the 1852 lectures, that the essence of university education is the cultivation of the intellect, and argues that the best instrument for cultivating the intellect is Greek and Roman literature. "The literature of Greece, continued into, and enriched by, the literature of Rome, together with the studies which it involves" (by these he means the traditional Liberal Arts: Music, Dialectics, Rhetoric, Grammar, Mathematics, Astronomy, Physics, and Geometry) "has been the instrument of education, and the food of civilization, from the first times of the world down to this day."[20] From time to time, Newman recognizes, this classical liberal arts education has been threatened, but "the instinct of Civilization and the common sense of Society" have always seen to it that classical studies "were acknowledged, as before, to be the best instruments of mental cultivation, and the best guarantees for intellectual progress."

Newman's justification of Classics as the core of liberal arts is more the work of a controversialist of genius than a sober historian. He was not thinking so much about John of Salisbury or other medieval critics of the Seven Liberal Arts as about the threats to Classics in his own age, and his appeal to "the instinct of Civilization and the common sense of Society" is as much prayer and persuasion as it is historical analysis.

In one way at least Newman's prayer failed, and his persuasive powers could not compete against social forces that would dissolve the instinct and common sense to which he appealed. He could sense the threat posed by the new sciences to the classical liberal arts' domination of the university curriculum, but he could write with confidence of the supremacy of Greek and Latin within the arts. In 1852 the social and cultural consensus to which Newman appealed was intact, unshaken by Marx, whose *Capital* did not appear until 1867, by Darwin, whose *On the Origin of Species by Means of Natural Selection* burst upon the world in 1859, or by the world wars that decimated the class Newman sought to educate. The classical authors had not yet been challenged on their own ground, and Newman could write that "Shakespeare and Milton are not studied in our course of education."[21] What he could not have foreseen was the democratization of education at all levels and the consequent fragmentation of the curriculum into a mob of subjects, all equal, all competing for a student's attention. As Newman was writing *The Idea of a University*, Charles Dickens was working on *Hard Times*. The repellent schoolmaster, Mr. McChoakumchild, with his head full of orthography, etymology, syntax, land-surveying, the watersheds of all the world, and twenty-three other subjects (Latin and Greek only two among them) and his heart full of nothing at all, is a better pointer to the future of education than John Henry Newman.

In another sense Newman succeeded, although in a way he could not have foreseen. By concentrating in the 1852 lectures on the aims and principles of liberal education rather than on the specifics of its curriculum, he enabled his idea of liberal arts to survive the collapse of the unified, humanistic classical education that had generated it and the dissolution of the structured society whose governing class classical education had originally been designed to form. Every time an educator argues for the importance of educating the whole student, or avoiding a too narrowly specialized and professional curriculum, or encouraging breadth and depth of studies, that educator is echoing Newman in a world Newman would not recognize or approve.

Classics survived the disappearance of Newman's world as only one among a host of liberal arts subjects. Many of them would seem distinctly strange to a resurrected Newman. Undergraduate courses in the History of Rock and Roll, Cowboys and Samurai, Oriental Rugs, Leisure Studies, and much else beside have all appeared under the rubric of liberal arts. But something of Newman's identification of liberal arts with Classics also survived. The same educators who echo Newman's ideas often point to Greek and Latin as examples of the kind of thing they mean by liberal arts, and there is, even now, a strong correlation between the quality of a university's Classics program and the quality of its commitment to liberal arts. Conservative and neoconservative polemicists, whose influence has waxed in recent years, find validation for their jeremiads in the state of Classics, even though they often seem to have grasped the wrong end of the right stick.[22]

It makes sense, then, for anyone who is interested in liberal arts education and a society's attitude toward it to look very carefully at the place of Classics in that society's educational system. Not only is it reasonable to suppose that the subject that Newman identified with liberal arts as he formulated the modern idea of them will be the surest indicator of their fate, but Newman's identification of liberal arts with Classics persists, in theory and in fact. What has happened to liberal arts can be seen most clearly by looking at what has happened to Classics. Or listening. Amid the babble that is modern American higher education, what youth's parsing or translation could make sense or harmony of a curriculum embracing Buddy Holly, *Middlemarch*, and the weavers of Khazan? An experienced ear, however, might catch a dominant note, the faint, echoing memory of the old grammar and the old paradigm.

ALTERTUMSWISSENSCHAFT

There is another reason to pay attention to Classics. It is ancestor and paradigm not only of liberal arts education, but also of something often set in opposition to it: research, and in particular scientific scholarship in the humanities.

Several generations of graduate students beginning their training in classical philology have heard the story of how Friedrich Augustus Wolf, when asked to sign the matriculation register at Göttingen in 1777, insisted on putting down *philologiae studiosus*, student of philology, rather than theology, law, or another recognized subject.[23] Wolf, the story goes, was a stubborn young man with a vision and a destiny. He went on to found the modern academic discipline known as classical philology, and his *Prolegomena ad Homerum* (1795) not only opened up the "Homeric Question" but was the first attempt to show the steps by which a classical text was handed down from the ancient world.[24]

Like most legends, the story of Wolf's matriculation does not survive the historian's sober examination. He was not the first to register as *philologiae studiosus*,[25] and the young man's clear vision of what lay ahead, as well as his stubbornness, may be a projection onto the great man's youth of his later accomplishments and mature personality. But, again like most legends, it ought to be true. Wolf is the central figure in an age of transition, and his work symbolizes, even if it did not cause, the crystallization of classical studies as a separate university subject and academic specialization. Before the early part of the nineteenth century, Classics so pervaded the curriculum that the study of Greek and Roman culture was not recognized as a single, separate subject. There was no professor of Latin as such at any British university until 1854, when John Conington became the first Corpus Professor of Latin at Oxford.[26] Until then, Latin had been a necessary tool for all university studies, not a separate object of research. During the early nineteenth century, in fact, the standard of classical teaching and scholarship may have been higher in elite secondary schools like Rugby and Winchester than in the universities to which they sent their students.[27] (Greek, of course, was different, a luxury "like lace," as Dr. Johnson remarked, and a subject with its own Regius Professors established at Oxford and Cambridge by Henry VIII.)

Two developments made the definition and demarcation of Classics in the nineteenth century necessary. One was the growing criticism of the uselessness of Latin and Greek as the sole content of education and the increasing pressure on the classical curriculum from other, modern subjects. Newman, as we have seen, was responding to these pressures. The other was the example set by a creation of nineteenth-century German universities, the idea of *Altertumswissenschaft*.

German scholars coined this word to replace the older term "philology" (*Philologie*). *Altertumswissenschaft* has no adequate English translation. "Science of antiquity" might do, but it is a bit ponderous, and most English-speaking classicists have simply added the German word to their vocabulary. Among American classicists *Altertumswissenschaft* has undergone a perversion similar to the one that has afflicted "literature" in other fields. When an American classical scholar complains of having to wade through a lot of *Wissenschaft* or *Altertumswissenschaft* on some question, the classicist means what a social scientist means by "the literature" of a subject: scholarly criticism and interpretation. There is also in this use of *Altertumswissenschaft* a hint that the scholarly writings in question are severely technical and probably a little dull.

As with "literature," the true meaning of *Altertumswissenschaft* is nobler than its colloquial degeneration. *Altertumswissenschaft* meant the study of Greco-Roman antiquity as a whole. Literature, philosophy, history, religion, art, architecture, daily life, the dialogues of Plato and the technical specifications of ancient Athenian plumbing, all were part of the unified study of the ancient world. Each part would illuminate the others and the whole.[28] That was not all. As Matthew Arnold saw, this study could lead as no other to knowledge of the self and of humanity: "To know himself, a man must know the capabilities and performances of the human spirit; the value of the humanities, of *Alterthumswissenschaft*, the science of antiquity, is that it affords for this purpose an unsurpassed source of light and stimulus."[29]

The idea of *Altertumswissenschaft* as a comprehensive study of antiquity was not without its antecedents. Like liberal arts education, it could trace its origin to the Renaissance and to humanist scholars like Politian or Lorenzo Valla, and before that perhaps to the encyclopedic scholars of Hellenistic Alexandria.[30] In the sixteenth century the great French scholar J. J. Scaliger spent the second half of his life in research upon the complicated and difficult texts of ancient chroniclers.[31] Ancient chronology may seem an unpromising subject, but few studies demand a more comprehensive knowledge of the ancient world or greater accuracy, learning, and intelligence. In the course of his work Scaliger argued that the history of the ancient world had to be understood as a whole, Greek, Roman, and Oriental, pagan and Christian together. Nearer Wolf's time, J. J. Winckelmann (1717–1768) showed the relationships between the beauties of Greek literature and the beauty of Greek sculpture and vase-painting, which was just then coming to the attention of western Europe. Winckelmann's ideas influenced not only scholars like Wolf and his teacher, Christian Gottlob Heyne, but also the neo-Hellenists and Romantic poets and artists of the late eighteenth and early nineteenth centuries in Germany and elsewhere. The still, pure, timeless Greeks and urns of Keats's "Ode" and Wedgewood pottery are Winckelmann's creation and monuments to the springs of *Altertumswissenschaft*.[32]

Those who followed Wolf developed and refined the concept of *Altertumswissenschaft*. One in particular, August Boeckh, grounded classical scholarship in German Idealist philosophy. Boeckh's *Encyclopedia and Methodology of the Philological Sciences*[33] of 1877 made it possible for *Altertumswissenschaft* to play a major role in educational thought and the development of the modern research university in the late nineteenth and early twentieth centuries. Boeckh, like Goethe and Hegel, argued that human thought was the finite realization of infinite, absolute ideas and that universal human ideas of concepts like art and beauty—or, perhaps, Art and Beauty—had found their first and best form in the achievements of Greek civilization.[34] Because those ideas were universal, a theory of the interpretation of classical antiquity would be, in Boeckh's view, a universal theory applicable to every product of the human mind. As Friedrich Schleiermacher had already shown, there was no need for separate methodologies for each kind of text; sacred and secular writings alike could be interpreted by the methods of classical scholarship.[35] Boeckh went even further; in his theory, classical philology became the pattern for every act of interpretation, including the most fundamental traffic in language between our minds and the world.

Boeckh's *Encyclopedia* falls into two parts. The first sets out a general theory of philological interpretation as recovery of an original idea, or as Boeckh puts it, the re-cognition of recognition;[36] interpretation, properly done, entails not merely reconstructing the past but also rethinking its thoughts. In the second part, Boeckh presents his philological reconstruction of antiquity. This reconstruction involves much more than secular literature and Scripture, the old provinces of philology. Classical philology now includes law and public life, private life, religion, the arts, mythology, philosophy, mathematics, and the natural sciences. It has become *Altertumswissenschaft*, a guide to the values of religion, social goods, beauty, truth, and other ideas.[37]

Little more than a century after Boeckh it is nearly impossible for us to recapture his sense that classical scholarship was a subject worth discussing at this level of philosophical abstraction and moral commitment. Interpretation theory takes Boeckh seriously but shows little more than polite interest in classical philology, mostly as historical curiosity.[38] The suggestion that studying Greek and Latin might guide us to important truths about human nature may seem plausible, if a bit overstated and old-fashioned, good rhetoric for commencement speeches or brochures to entice undergraduates to major in Greek. The contention that classical studies is not one way among many, but the best way, even the only way, to these truths seems little short of lunacy. Yet this astonishing contention guided not only Boeckh, but his successors in the generation of Wilamowitz and Nietzsche.

No scholar writes in a vacuum. By hinting at Boeckh's affinity to Hegel, I have done no more than recognize the obvious influence of German Idealist philosophy on his picture of classical scholarship. Political circumstances also had a part to play. The half-century between the death of Wolf and Boeckh's *Encyclopedia* saw the rise of a unified Germany and the development of its national consciousness. The new German universities played an important role in this development, and their shape and priorities owed much to the advocates of *Altertumswissenschaft*, prominent among them Wilhelm von Humboldt, philologist and Prussian minister of education.[39] Nor should we forget that the foundation text of *Altertumswissenschaft*, Wolf's *Prolegomena to Homer*, drew much of its approach and methodology from J. B. Eichhorn's studies of the text of the Hebrew Bible and shared theological studies' sense that Scripture could be exposed to the light of historical criticism.[40] It shared, also, theology's sense that the application of philological methods could produce answers to central questions.

This central place of classical scholarship in nineteenth-century German thought proceeds from the conviction, seen at its clearest in Boeckh, that *Altertumswissenschaft* asks important questions and offers answers that go beyond mere antiquarianism. Science—or as we naturally say now, even science—might pattern itself on classical philology, as the philosopher Schelling supposed: "In geology we still await the genius who will analyze the earth and show its composition as Wolf analyzed Homer."[41] Philology may even have perfected, as Daniel Dennett notes, the "characteristically Darwinian" argument from homology before Darwin, as the founder of evolution himself recognized.[42]

For more than a century now, since 1883 when Conrad Bursian published his *History of Classical Philology in Germany*,[43] those who think about the history of classical scholarship have distinguished two approaches to the subject. One can be traced, primarily through German scholars and those trained in the German tradition, to Boeckh, K. O. Müller, and before them to Wolf and Winckelmann. It is aesthetic, historical, and archaeological, concerned with things as well as with words; as Wolf himself observed, the arts must be loved, but history must be revered. The other approach is literary and linguistic, philological in the narrow sense. It runs through A. E. Housman, the German scholar Gottfried Hermann, and Richard Bentley to the humanist scholars of the Renaissance, and it concerns itself especially with exact analysis of the ancient languages and with textual criticism, the craft of disentangling an ancient text's words from the errors and corruptions brought about by centuries of copying and recopying by the hands of scribes. Bitter disputes between Boeckh and Hermann and between Müller and Hermann helped to shape emerging *Altertumswissenschaft* in the first half of the nineteenth century.[44]

Like most dichotomies, the division of classical scholarship into the disciples of Boeckh and the disciples of Hermann oversimplifies a confused reality. It might be more accurate to see three traditions: the Idealist, represented by Boeckh, Wilamowitz, and the other practitioners of Boeckh's comprehensive, aesthetic *Altertumswissenschaft*; the Empiricist, represented by the language-centered studies of Housman and British philology; and the Humanist, an essentially educational tradition, which we have seen summed up in Newman. At every stage, however, the traditions intertwine and cross-pollinate, and no scholar or piece of scholarship shows an uncontaminated pedigree. There is a further complication: the traditions themselves are no longer generally understood and have been infiltrated or replaced by false and corrupt versions of their true selves.

But it is the first tradition that dominates American graduate schools, and not only in departments of Classics. Just as the third tradition, the Humanist, as articulated by Newman, was the inspiration for the liberal arts curricula of American undergraduate education, so German *Altertumswissenschaft*, sometimes in an uneasy tension with an essentially British philology, shaped American graduate programs. The founders of the Johns Hopkins University, the first American school to offer doctoral degrees based on substantial work in non-professional subjects, patterned their new institution on the German universities where they had studied.[45] The only nonscientist among its five original faculty members, professor of Greek Basil Lanneau Gildersleeve, had been a student of Boeckh at Berlin.[46] The Ph.D. degree, the seminar—an invention of Wolf's predecessor at Göttingen, J. M. Gesner—the dissertation, all the formal apparatus of graduate education in this country, originated in the advanced classical curricula of nineteenth-century German universities.[47]

Nearly every professor of English or Urdu, French or physics, in an American university has received graduate training patterned on the nineteenth-century model of training in *Altertumswissenschaft*. Nearly every university or college teacher, even if he or she has no scholarly ambitions and never publishes a line or thinks a thought, in some measure inherits a tradition going back to Wolf and Gesner, and to the study of that ancient world in which Boeckh and his followers found the key to all that was true and beautiful in human life.

THE FALSE PARADIGMS

Two authentic paradigms, liberal arts education and *Altertumswissenschaft*, organized the grammar of civility that was classical education. In university departments of Classics today, their names occur in praise or invocation. The insular folk touch the dials made of seashells and move the antennas made of palm fronds, just as they always have, in just the way that once worked. But both paradigms have vanished. They have been replaced by false paradigms, the grammar of a language in which it is impossible to make true statements about anything but the grammar itself.

The False Liberal Arts

From its beginning in the Renaissance, liberal arts education was classical, humanistic, and Christian, designed to educate members of the governing classes by acquainting them with the best patterns of conduct, modes of thinking, and products of culture. Newman added a further, Platonic, refinement: in liberal arts education, knowledge was sought for its own sake, not for its usefulness in any specific profession or endeavor. This liberal arts education existed in the service of a governing class. I am not interested here in arguing the advantages or moral rightness of such a class; the fact is, someone governs in every society, and in western European and American society from the Renaissance to the First World War, those who did were, almost without exception, the products of an education dominated by the classical, liberal arts paradigm.

Then they were gone. Again, this is no place to attempt an explanation of their disappearance. The old governing class did not so much disappear as shatter. The growth, flourishing, and finally the unquestioned
triumph of democracy made it impossible to reassemble the fragments. If
the authority of government comes from all the people and from all kinds
of people, then society must be open to every language of civility. There
must be not a single grammar, classical education, but as many grammars
as there are ideas of civic good. As Amy Gutmann puts it,

> No set of virtues remains undisputed in the United States, or in any
> modern society that allows its members to dispute its dominant under-
> standings. The problem in using education to bias children towards
> some conceptions of the good life and away from others stems not
> from pretense on the part of educators to moral superiority over chil-
> dren but from an assertion on their part to political authority over
> other citizens who reject their conception of virtue.[48]

To suggest that those who will govern need a special kind of education
is to question the basic premise of democracy, that all men and women
are by nature equally fit to take part in governing. Indeed, since education (not merely what schools are attended, but what stories are told,
what images seen) defines a class by creating its self-consciousness, to
design an education for a governing class subverts democracy.

The necessary openness of thought in a democracy has a consequence that is fatal to the paradigm of classical liberal arts education. In
a democratic society, the freedom and theoretical equality of all citizens
make it necessary to avoid privileging any single set of beliefs or ideas.
But to discover that one idea or belief makes better sense than another
is to create a case for replacing the one making less sense. In a democracy, therefore, powerful impulses urge the avoidance of argumentation.
Arguments we have in plenty, but orderly comparison and judgment of
beliefs and ideas are rare. In a modern democratic society, as Alasdair
MacIntyre observes, "the apparent assertion of principles functions as a
mask for expressions of personal preferences,"[49] and in matters of taste,
as the proverb says, there can be no disputing.

Yet the comparison and judgment of beliefs and the imposition of better instead of worse were at the center of classical liberal arts education. At the end of his seventh *Discourse on The Idea of a University*, Newman set out what his ideal education would do in society:

> It aims at raising the intellectual tone of society, at cultivating the public mind, at purifying the national taste, at supplying true principles to popular enthusiasm and fixed aims to popular aspiration, at giving enlargement and sobriety to the ideas of the age, at facilitating the exercise of political power, and refining the intercourse of private life. It is the education which gives a man a clear conscious view of his own opinions and judgements, a truth in developing them, an eloquence in expressing them and a force in urging them. It teaches him to see things as they are, to go right to the point, to disentangle a skein of thought, to detect what is sophistical, and to discard what is irrelevant.[50]

It is, in fact, the education of an enlightened and undemocratic governing class that will cultivate and purify even as it restrains and moderates the enthusiasms and aspirations of the people.

In the ideal of classical liberal education, judgment, discrimination, and evaluation of ideas were essential to the social function of classically and liberally educated people. The instrument through which they were to judge, distinguish, and evaluate ideas was language; and clearness, accuracy, and precision in using language were at every period goals of liberal arts education. "Composition" —that is, translation of prose or verse from a vernacular language into Latin or Greek—and other exercises designed to develop these skills became part of the teaching of the classical languages on which liberal education was based.

Clearness, accuracy, and precision, however, may not be virtues of language in a democratic society, especially if that society is a modern, bureaucratic nation-state. Democratic ideals of freedom and equality demand respect for the ideas and beliefs of other people, and it is difficult, though a democratic saint might manage it, to have respect for an opinion known to be wrong. In most people's minds, equality of persons implies equality of beliefs and opinions. In these conditions, the use of language to judge, discriminate, and evaluate opinions will be discouraged. It may even seem anti-democratic, elitist, or excessively intellectual. Thus in a 1980 presidential debate between Ronald Reagan and Jimmy Carter, Carter's fact-heavy, closely argued refutation of the Republican position on Medicare had no chance against Reagan's folksy, anti-intellectual "There you go again!" George W. Bush, who was articulate and eloquent when he was running for governor of Texas, had to discover the advantages of being inarticulate when he sought higher office.[51]

In a bureaucracy, also, the linguistic virtues imparted by classical liberal education will be disadvantages. Any suggestion that an unelected governing class exists in a democracy is to be deprecated or denied. Bureaucrats, who form such a class, gain power and longevity by rejecting any imputation that their actions are based on individual acts of judgment, discrimination, or evaluation.[52] They claim effectiveness, efficiency, and an ability to predict events based on what are seen as necessary laws of human behavior, impersonally interpreted. Yet clarity, even by something as simple as establishing a preference for active verbs, may compel an official to acknowledge his individual responsibility. Accuracy and precision may leave little room for future maneuver or negotiated compromise. Even the bureaucrat's note to his subordinate begins "From the desk of . . ." and so insulates the author from his words. In Newman's world, furniture did not talk.

Although Newman knew that careful instruction in Latin and Greek was the best way to develop the linguistic virtues attendant upon classical liberal education, in his *Idea of a University* he carefully avoided specifying a curriculum. In so doing he not only made it possible for the ideal of liberal arts education to survive the disappearance of the governing class it had created and served, he also made possible the adaptation of his elitist liberal arts to the democratic and bureaucratic societies that replaced the one he knew. All that was necessary was that the old ideals of clarity, accuracy, and precision be replaced by a new, egalitarian sense of the relation between statements and the world in which liberally educated people lived.

Newman argued that liberal arts education is distinguished from other educations not by *what* subject is studied, but by *how* it is studied. His contention that liberal arts education is defined by the seeking of knowledge for its own sake made it possible for those who came after him to assume that some kinds of knowledge other than classical studies might be liberal arts if they were studied for their own sake. It became evident, also, that there were in fact many subjects as important as Classics had always been. If a student could be liberally educated in Newman's sense, and at the same time know as much about thermodynamics as his grandfather had known about Latin prose composition, then surely society was better off.

It is but a short step from the recognition that some subjects may be liberal arts subjects to the notion that any subject may be a liberal arts subject. This notion interlocks with and is reinforced by the democratic belief in the equality of opinions to create the false paradigm of liberal arts education, which prevails in American universities little more than a century after Newman. In this paradigm, "liberal arts" is defined negatively. The liberal arts are not sciences, and so a university may have a College of Natural Sciences and a College of Liberal Arts. The liberal arts are not mathematical, and college courses in quantitative subjects often exist in two versions, one with mathematics for premeds and other serious students and one without, for liberal arts types. The liberal arts are not vocational. Courses in accounting or engineering belong somewhere other than in a liberal arts college. And, inevitably in a society that values the scientific, mathematical, and pragmatic, the liberal arts are not serious. They are decorations for life, high-class activities for the leisure time of an expensively educated person. Like the expensive German car and the understated furniture, they establish him or her as a person who has good taste to go with the money.

In talking about these nonscientific, nonmathematical, nonvocational subjects, the false paradigm suggests, we are not talking about anything very serious, nor are we talking very seriously. Statements in the realm of liberal arts—aesthetic judgments, literary criticism, moral analysis—do not have the rigor of scientific fact or mathematical proof.

If they did, we might have to act on them or defer to the experts who have been educated to make them with clearness, accuracy, and precision, with consequences inimical to democracy.

There are two responses to the observation, which Plato was probably the first to make,[53] that we can be more certain in speaking about some kinds of things than about others. One response devalues discourse on subjects about which certainty is impossible and makes that discourse less important and less worth attention than discourse on subjects where certain knowledge is possible. It is satisfying to know why airplanes fly or to have hopes of discovering a cure for cancer, and society holds such knowledge in high regard. It frustrates many people to think that there can be no agreement on what a poem means, or even whether poems have meanings. Nearly everyone outside today's universities, and most of those inside, respond to the liberal arts with some measure of frustration or suspicion. If one's children propose to major in a liberal arts subject, it is usual to caution them against such impractical notions and to advise them to make sure that in addition to their knowledge of Greek and poetry they have a way to learn a living.

The other response seeks a way to claim that discourse on subjects where certainty is unattainable is worthy of the same consideration as discourse on subjects where it is. This response, naturally enough, prevails among advocates of the liberal arts. Their version of it, however, avoids the argumentatively suicidal frontal attack of asserting that discourse on art, literature, or morals is just as true and true in just the same way as discourse on science or mathematics. Instead, the advocates of liberal arts outflank their antagonists. They claim that their discourse is true, but true in a different way, or that discourse on scientific and mathematical subjects, or even all discourse, shares in the inexact nature of discourse on art or literature.

This counterclaim, made in opposition to the scientific and mathematical idea of truth that dominates our age, takes several forms, ranging from the sophomore's naïve claim that his professor's criticism of his paper is "just an opinion" to the most rarefied heights of linguistics and philosophy. Its extreme, perhaps its ultimate development (here I exaggerate and simplify, as careful readers will notice) comes with the rejection of reference by semiology and deconstructionism. According to these doctrines every decoding of a statement, every unraveling of language to find meaning, is in fact another encoding, another weaving of a web called a text. If we believe that the wily serpent of language forever swallows its tail as it grows, it becomes impossible to talk about anything. All talk, even the scientist's laws, is talk about talk.

One would think that classical scholars would leap at this way of knowing. After all, their texts give the appearance of being about a world that has vanished forever, one which has no reference outside our description of it. A sentence of Cicero is not about anything in our world or even in a language that any of us now claims as his native tongue, and our only hope of interpreting it lies in relating it to other utterances in Latin or Greek. Yet, with a few exceptions, classical scholars have not jumped to embrace the deconstructionist paradigm. Indeed, it would be hard to find an academic discipline in the humanities more inclined to be suspicious of postmodern linguistics and literary criticism than Classics. But the professors of Classics show no great interest in defending liberal arts. Instead they, or most of them, have cast their lot with the second false paradigm.

The False Altertumswissenschaft

Why the professors of Classics shy away from the suggestion that all language is self-referential and that "meaning" is an elusive and problematic concept remains unclear. Perhaps to most of them—busy people who want to get on with publications and the careers that publications create—theorizing seems merely a distraction. Deconstructionist approaches, also, may seem to threaten something seen as fundamental to Classics. If a text, once it is deconstructed, disappears, then it becomes impossible to justify any particular identity or special status for Classics, since classical texts by definition are those that persistently fail to disappear. Or perhaps an accident of history condemned American classicists to an arid and unreflective historical positivism. When the founders of American graduate schools went to Germany, they found German universities already rigidly departmentalized. German classical scholarship in the 1860s and 1870s, also, was dominated by a concern for the discovery, analysis, and classification of hard facts about the ancient world. The German professors who taught the first generation of American professional classicists were not themselves much interested in theoretical questions about meaning and interpretation. "American students" in Germany, wrote Basil Gildersleeve to the President of Johns Hopkins, "are too prone to acquire the undesirable sides of German work and become more German than the Germans in their mode of presentation, in the cumbrousness of their apparatus, in the thinness of conclusions as compared with the thickness of material, in a certain routine criticism, which well-known models have made a mere mechanical process." Gildersleeve went on to hope for a return to the comprehensive vision of Boeckh; meanwhile, American graduate schools were being founded and staffed by those Ph.D.s "more German than the Germans."[54]

There may be yet another reason for American classicists' reluctance to think about how their subject has meaning and for their prevalent disdain for questions about the theory of their discipline. The classical scholars, without knowing it, have taken sides in a conflict of giants that defined *Altertumswissenschaft* for the twentieth century. Like anyone who comes late to a fight, they have found it difficult to see the original issues clearly.[55]

NIETZSCHE AND WILAMOWITZ

The first thing to remember is that the principal antagonists were very young in 1872. Friedrich Nietzsche was twenty-seven; Ulrich von Wilamowitz-Moellendorff was four years younger. That difference of four years had not kept them from rivalry during their school days at Pforte, the ancient Prussian boarding school whose influence on German cultural life can be compared to that of Eton or Winchester in England. To the then thirteen- or fourteen-year-old Wilamowitz, Nietzsche would have seemed a reputation and a rival. The older boy, perhaps already aware of his own genius, may have seen Wilamowitz as an intelligent but conventional aristocrat, the sort of boy who won all the prizes because he knew how to please the masters.[56]

The antagonism persisted even after both young men had begun to make their careers in university teaching and classical scholarship. Nietzsche did not bother to set down any precise account of his personal feelings toward Wilamowitz. When their quarrel took place, after all, Nietzsche looked down from the chair of Classics at Basel while Wilamowitz had only just completed his doctorate. Later, Nietzsche left *Altertumswissenschaft* for the higher and smoother road of his own thought, and finally he went mad.

It is possible, however, to discover two reasons for Wilamowitz's dislike of Nietzsche. First, as students at the University of Bonn he and Nietzsche had taken opposite sides in an internecine conflict between two members of the classical faculty, Friedrich Ritschl and Otto Jahn. The two professors' enmity had blossomed from a simple disagreement over the appointment of a third academic, Hermann Sauppe, into a full-blown hatred, waged with the passion and intensity that great minds sometimes give to small matters. As often happens in such academic quarrels, one combatant retired from the field. Ritschl left Bonn for Leipzig, and shortly thereafter Nietzsche went there also. Although the musical life of Leipzig, where he would fall under the spell of Wagner, attracted Nietzsche at least as much as the presence of his old teacher, Wilamowitz was sufficiently ardent a partisan to regard Ritschl's apparent ally as Jahn's enemy.

A second, far more important reason sprang from Wilamowitz's sense of fairness. In this matter it is important to move away from the vantage point that we gain from hindsight. Because we know that Nietzsche was one of the most influential thinkers of the late nineteenth century, we tend to assume that every early recognition of his genius was no more than a statement of the obvious. How would Friedrich Nietzsche have appeared to his contemporaries, or near contemporaries, in 1872?

He might have seemed to be a young man who had been advanced far beyond his deserts by an academic establishment all too ready to be impressed by showy imitations of genius or willingness to become the client of some great academic patron. At Pforte, Nietzsche had failed mathematics, and his graduation was at risk. Classics was his subject, and Wilhelm Corssen, the Classics master, had a word with the mathematics master: "Do you perhaps want us to allow the most gifted student that the school has had since I have been here to fail?" Nietzsche passed.

After Nietzsche joined Ritschl at Leipzig, the professor assiduously promoted his young colleague's career. In 1865, while he was still at Bonn, Nietzsche had helped to found a university classical society, the Philologischer Verein, and at its meeting in January 1866, he presented a paper on the formation of the *Theognidea*, a collection of archaic Greek poetry attributed to the poet Theognis. Ritschl was so impressed that he invited Nietzsche to publish the paper in *Rheinisches Museum*, the classical journal that Ritschl edited. Thereafter *Rheinisches Museum* always had a place for Nietzsche's articles.

In 1867, when the University of Basel solicited nominations for a recently vacated chair of classical philology, Ritschl submitted a panegyric of his favorite student. Its glowing terms won Nietzsche the appointment at the astonishingly early age of twenty-four, before he had even completed his doctorate. Ritschl obligingly saw to it that Nietzsche was excused from the comprehensive examination and dissertation and awarded a doctorate on the grounds of his previously published work in *Rheinisches Museum*. Wilamowitz was not the only one to wonder at this circle of self-fulfilling laudation.

The young Nietzsche, in fact, Nietzsche the rising classical scholar, the *Wunderkind* who had not yet written his first book, must have appeared to many of his contemporaries as a careerist who owed his position less to his scholarly merits than to his limpetlike attachment to Ritschl and his ability to impress men like Corssen. The patrons were right, of course, though not about Nietzsche's classical scholarship. The youthful articles promise well, but no more.[57] If they had been written by a scholar ten years older, no one would have thought them remarkable. There was something there, something that would become the greatness of Nietzsche, but—and the point needs emphasis—there was no justification for Nietzsche's meteoric early career in classical philology. To a disinterested observer, and still more to an interested one of the opposite party, Nietzsche in 1872 had much to live up to.

The young scholar's first book, *The Birth of Tragedy out of the Spirit of Music* (*Die Geburt der Tragödie aus dem Geiste der Musik*), rolled off the presses in the last days of 1871 and was distributed to bookstores early in 1872. Ritschl received a copy before anyone else, and Nietzsche saw to it that copies went to Richard Wagner, whose ideas on music and drama had captured his imagination and who was coming to replace Ritschl as an intellectual father figure, to Cosima Wagner, and to a few friends in the community of classical scholars—though not, as William M. Calder III has pointed out, to the senior professors most competent to judge its value as a study of Greek tragedy.[58] Here at last was something by which to test the claims of Nietzsche's advance billing.

At first, *The Birth of Tragedy* attracted few buyers and little notice. But in February 1872, Rudolf Schöll, a junior member of the classical faculty at the University of Berlin, suggested to a new friend of his, Ulrich von Wilamowitz-Moellendorff, that if Wilamowitz would write a review of the new book, Schöll could see that it was published in the *Göttingischer gelehrte Anzeigen*, an important scholarly journal with a history stretching back to 1739. Wilamowitz's contempt for the jumped-up professor of Basel may have been obvious. Everyone knew that Wilamowitz had stood with Otto Jahn in the quarrel with Ritschl, and Nietzsche's blast against Jahn in section 19 of *The Birth of Tragedy* made it likely on the face of things that Wilamowitz would produce a negative review in defense of his beloved teacher. Schöll had reason to welcome a harsh evaluation of Nietzsche's first book, for he had been one of the nominees passed over when Nietzsche was appointed at Basel.

Wilamowitz later wondered if Schöll's suggestion had been a joke, but at the time it was made he did not hesitate to carry it out. In March of 1872, during a fortnight's vacation at his family's home in Posen, he drafted his review. The Göttingen journal declined to publish it, and in April, back in Berlin after two weeks' military service, Wilamowitz, again prompted by Schöll, revised it and arranged its publication as a booklet at his own expense. On May 30, 1872, appeared *Futurephilology! A Reply to "The Birth of Tragedy" of Friedrich Nietzsche, Professor at Basel, by Ulrich von Wilamowitz-Moellendorff, Ph.d.*[59] The storm had broken.

Futurephilology!'s title mocks Wagner's *Zukunftsmusik*. Its title page cites an obscure fragment of Aristophanes to the effect that exquisite cuisine (like, presumably, Nietzsche's trendy rhetoric) is "just buggery compared to a big piece of meat." When Wilamowitz exposes an error of a few centuries in Nietzsche's dating of an ancient proverb, he glee-fully trowels on the irony. Surely, he writes, one would hope that the masters of Pforte would have kept to Plato's dictum about denying the unmathematical entrance to the temple of philosophy—or at least denied them exit. Wilamowitz knew about Nietzsche's narrow escape from the toils of Pforte's mathematics department. The pamphlet closed with a demand that Nietzsche give up his pretense of teaching *Altertumswissenschaft* at Basel.

Nietzsche composed no reply to *Futurephilology!* but left that task to his friends, Wagner and the philologist Erwin Rohde. In June 1872, Wagner entered the fray with a letter in the *Norddeutsche Allgemeine Zeitung*. Rohde published his counterblast, *Posteriorphilology* (*Philology to the Rear*—the anal pun is there in German as well), in October. Wilamowitz came back with *Zukunftsphilologie! II* in 1873. Then other, more important matters summoned the combatants from the struggle.

This bit of academic controversy, whose complications I have only sketched, shows features that recur in the quarrels of university folk. Patronage, undeserved promotion and the resentment or incensed love of justice that it arouses, the rigged review, and the personal attacks, will all be familiar to anyone who has spent any time in academic life. The conflict between Nietzsche and Wilamowitz epitomizes the way in which friendships, animosities, and ambitions give color, even if they do not provide shape and outline, to every scholar's work. All good schol-arship is as passionate as poetry, and the best of it has something of great poetry's transformation of personal history into truth.[60]

If only because it presents an exemplary case of these issues, the quarrel of Nietzsche and Wilamowitz is important. But it also came at a time when the concept of *Altertumswissenschaft* had reached a kind of acme and was about to produce in the mature Wilamowitz its greatest genius and in Nietzsche the prophet of its decline. Their dispute and the reactions of contemporary and later observers reveal the roots of the false *Altertumswissenschaft* that by a century later had strangled the noble growth.

Insofar as their conflict was about Greek drama, Wilamowitz was right and victorious. *The Birth of Tragedy* attracts readers because it is a profound and powerful meditation on the springs of tragic art in the human spirit and because it offers an important thinker's early views on art, music, Greek civilization, and other subjects of equal importance. No one, however, who wants to know what Greek tragic drama was like or how to read it will find help in Nietzsche, who may have written *The Birth of Tragedy* without having read much more than Euripides *Bacchae*.[61] Serious students of Greek theater still discover valuable insights in Wilamowitz's *Introduction to Greek Tragedy* of 1889. The *Birth of Tragedy*, like Aristotle's *Poetics* and Horace's *Ars Poetica*, is a great and influential aesthetic treatise based on an idiosyncratic misunderstanding of the nature of Greek tragedy.

But the accuracy and utility of Nietzsche's comments on Greek tragedy are beside the point. He and Wilamowitz, as both men recognized later in their lives, were not speaking the same language. The discourse of the poet and prophet could not be criticized by using the grammar of *Altertumswissenschaft*. The aged Wilamowitz was content to leave to another tribunal final judgment on Nietzsche's prophetic utterances: "Whether his self-deification and his blasphemies against Socrates and Christ will win him victory, that is the future's lesson."[62]

Wilamowitz's priorities in blasphemy reveal something about his objection to Nietzsche and point to a way in which Nietzsche's prophecies were fulfilled. Wilamowitz, who once gave his religion as *fides Platonica* (the religion of Plato), found in Nietzsche's discussion of Socrates at sections 13–15 of *The Birth of Tragedy* more than error or inaccuracy. He found blasphemy, to be denounced in the same breath as and ahead of blasphemy against Christ.

In his account of Socrates, Nietzsche accurately diagnoses a problem. He has exaggerated and rhapsodized it, as he was to do later with his announcement of the death of God, but from his dithyrambic style emerges a clear and undespairing revelation of the point at which *Altertumswissenschaft* becomes futile.

For Nietzsche, Socrates is the type of "the Theoretical Man" who "finds an infinite delight in whatever exists."[63] This delight protects the Theoretical Man from the artist's despair at the inevitable limitations of knowledge and at the same time makes it impossible for him to share the artist's profound understanding of the surfaces of things. While Nietzsche wrote, squadrons of anonymous philologists, the dwarves of *Altertumswissenschaft*, were toiling to mine the gold of antiquity and display it in great collective works of learning like the *Corpus Inscriptionum Latinarum*, which had begun to appear in 1863 under the direction of Wilamowitz's mentor (and future father-in-law), Theodor Mommsen. Nietzsche's description of the ecstatic burrowings of the Theoretical Men in their search for the goddess Truth resembles nothing so much as an Aristophanic burlesque of the specialized, complementary, and self-replacing labors of Socratic *Altertumswissenschaft*.

> There would be no science [*Wissenschaft*] if it were concerned only with that one nude goddess and with nothing else. For in that case her devotees would have to feel like men who wanted to dig a hole straight through the earth, assuming that each of them realized that even if he tried his utmost, his whole life long, he would only be able to dig a very small portion of this enormous depth, and even that would be filled in again before his own eyes by the labors of the next in line, so a third person would seem to do well if he picked a new spot for his drilling efforts.

During the first six months of 1875 Nietzsche turned his attention to an analysis of the state of his profession, which he intended would form part of a larger whole titled *Untimely Meditations* (*Unzeitgemasse*

Betrachtungen).[64] He never progressed further than setting down a series of aphoristic notes for "We Philologists" ("Wir Philologen"), but from these fragments we can gain an understanding of what a man like Wilamowitz would have found objectionable in the hints and indirections of *The Birth of Tragedy*. The scholars' quarrel was more than personal, and more than an academic disagreement over how to understand Greek tragedy. The anger that Wilamowitz felt toward Nietzsche was the anger of a priest and doctor of the Church toward an apostate, and the two men's most fundamental disagreement was over the true state of the discipline to which each had dedicated his life.

"We Philologists" focuses on the contrast between the object of philology, which for Nietzsche is less the entire ancient world than simply classical Greek antiquity, and the moral and intellectual condition of those who profess philology. Nietzsche's Greeks stand as examples whose moral clarity it is impossible to imitate. The attempt produces despair if one is an artist and ridiculousness if one is a philologue. It is hard to take this line of analysis very seriously, since there is no evidence that, say, reading the *Iliad* produces or ought to produce heroism, any more than reading the New Testament produces Christianity or *Madame Bovary*, adultery. From Plato onward, moralists have underestimated and oversimplified the witchery of literature.

But Nietzsche has a point when he insists on the essentially moral nature of the Greek example and of education based on it. He reserves his sharpest condemnation for classical scholars as educators and for the undeserved primacy of classical studies in the education of his day. He sums up the reasons for the preference given to Classics as "ignorance, mistaken judgements, and sophistic conclusions" on the one hand and "the professional self-interest of the philologists" on the other. In a passage that seems genuinely prophetic when read while waiting for a meeting of the diminished and irrelevant Classics department of some modern university, he foretells the fate of classical studies in the century since he wrote:

> Actually the reasons for this preference are now gradually disappearing, and if the fact has not been noticed by philologists, it has been

noted with maximum clarity outside their circle. The study of history has had its effect; then linguistics caused an enormous defection—and even desertion—among the philologists. Now all they have left is the schools; but for how long? In the form in which it has existed until now, classical philology is dying out: the ground has vanished from under it. Whether philologists will survive as a profession is extremely doubtful; in any case they are a dying race.[65]

Nietzsche saw that the life was draining away from the *Altertums-wissenschaft* founded by Wolf. Boeckh himself had already recognized the tendency to partition in his concept of *Altertumswissenschaft*, and his division of philology into a formal or theoretical part and a material part attempts to unify the various subdisciplines under a comprehensive theory of knowledge. Yet Boeckh acknowledged that antiquity itself, the very matter of philology, was far from uniform, and that its unity in the philologist's eyes was an ideal never to be realized in practice.[66] Already in 1875 the interesting questions were coming from other fields. Wolf's and Boeckh's ideal of a comprehensive science of antiquity had yielded to the demand for specialized research. If it was impossible to know enough about everything ancient, it would at least be possible to know everything about something. The mansion that was our knowledge of the ancient world would be constructed brick by brick, and each scholar would contribute according to his ability. Some could supply a single brick ("A Textual Problem in Book XXII of Livy"), some a section of wall ("The Chronology of Hannibal's March into Italy"), some a room (*Rome and Carthage*) or more.[67] Yet the founders of this noble ideal were already out of date, part of the last wave of Renaissance polymathy before it broke on the rocks of modern scientific speculation. Even to make a simple brick in the mansion of *Altertumswissenschaft* needed skills that could take an intelligent man a lifetime to master, and as the structure grew ever larger, it became less and less likely that any single person could master more than a few feet of wall.

Nietzsche the perceptive observer and analyst of the intellectual situation of his time understood that *Altertumswissenschaft* could not preserve the moral ideal of Boeckh and the central place in culture given it by Wolf so long as it modeled itself on the craft of brickmakers rather than the visions of architects. Historicism and the positivist emphasis on fact often seemed to endorse the belief that getting a date wrong was worse than misunderstanding an ethical situation posed by the ancient world. In "We Philologists" Nietzsche rejects Boeckh's ideal unity of antiquity and hints at the possibility of revitalizing philology by taking a radically clear-sighted look at the Greeks without the distorting mirrors of Roman antiquity, Christianity, or the traditions of classical education, and in *The Birth of Tragedy* he dares to hope that such a fresh look will restore to the Greeks their place as patterns for the tragic sense of existential despair in which he centered true morality.

To Wilamowitz, this was nonsense, and unnecessary nonsense at that. He could not believe that *Altertumswissenschaft* had been separated from the vital center of contemporary art and literature or that classical scholarship would inevitably withdraw into a narrow and lifeless world of its own. How could it, when for him the study of the ancient world was essential, vital, and demanding?

Perhaps no passage from Wilamowitz's writings is more often quoted than an image he presented at a lecture in Oxford on June 3, 1908:

> The tradition is dead; our task is to revivify life that has passed away.
> We know that ghosts cannot speak until they have drunk blood; and
> the spirits which we evoke demand the blood of our hearts. We give it
> to them gladly; but if they then abide our question, something from us
> has entered into them; something alien, that must be cast out, cast out
> in the name of truth!

Wilamowitz is not saying that our study of the ancient world should be bloodless or impersonal. For him, scholarship demands nothing less than heroic struggle between passion and objectivity. He had already used the Homeric image of the philologist's blood as a sacrifice revitalizing the dry spirits of antiquity in the conclusion of his *Introduction to Greek Tragedy* of 1889:

It is a matter of being absorbed into another's soul, be it that of an individual or of a people. In the offering up of our own individuality lies our strength. We philologists as such have nothing of the poet or of the prophet, both of which the historian should be to a certain degree. On the other hand we should bear something of the actor in us, not of the star performer who uses a role to set forth his talents, but of the true artist, who gives life to the dead words through his own heart's blood.[68]

No wonder Wilamowitz hated Nietzsche. They were so much alike: passionately devoted to the contemplation of the ancient world and convinced that the impulse to study it was a vocation, not a profession. But Ulrich von Wilamowitz-Moellendorff, the proud aristocrat who had taught himself humility because he knew that only by effacing the self could he approach the Greeks he loved, looked at Nietzsche and saw vanity, egotism, and an actor who interpreted himself and betrayed his role. Worse, impressionable people listened to him and were enticed from the true path. Shortly after Nietzsche's death on August 25, 1900, Wilamowitz made public reference to him:

> But now we see numerous young people going astray, and many falling, because they have been seduced by a dangerous philosophy or semi-philosophy, in fact by Nietzsche.[69]

Nietzsche was not only a traitor to *Altertumswissenschaft*; he was a dangerous charlatan and a corrupter of youth, guilty in fact of the crimes with which the Athenians had falsely charged Socrates. Nietzsche's guilt made his blasphemy against Wilamowitz's beloved Socrates all the more contemptible.

Eastern and Western Christianity separated over a difference about the nature of Christ that could be expressed by inserting or omitting an iota from a single Greek word. Like many intellectual disputes between parties of similar backgrounds and shared premises, the quarrel between Nietzsche and Wilamowitz quickly grew into schism. Later adherents magnified differences of detail and exaggerated their importance. The sense that *Altertumswissenschaft* was a demanding and essentially moral vocation rather than a career came to seem Nietzschean, and therefore loony, to the followers of Wilamowitz. Nietzsche soon broke all ties with the world of university teaching, and his attempts to reform a technical academic discipline seemed irrelevant. The common ground vanished, and a false paradigm of *Altertumswissenschaft* held the field nearly unchallenged.

This false *Altertumswissenschaft* has no room for Wilamowitz's heroic tension between the revitalizing personal commitment to the ancient world and the suppression of personality in order to win the goal of truth.[70] It has none of Wilamowitz's conviction that what the Greeks and Romans say to us depends on what we give to them.

Instead the false paradigm holds out the illusion that the ancient world has an existence independent of its observers and can be accurately described. The value of a scholar's statements depends on how well they match what is seen as the reality of Greece and Rome. These absolute statements derive their value not only from their accuracy in describing Greek and Roman culture but also from their lack of any connection to their author or his culture. The ideal work of scholarship is one so weakly connected to its own time and so strongly connected to the ancient world that its statements remain true, and its value intact, forever.

Some kinds of statements have a better chance of meeting these criteria than others. The publication of the text of an inscription, for example, is more likely to retain value of this kind than is a critical analysis of *Oedipus the King*. As a classicist's discourse about antiquity becomes more engaged, personal, and interpretative, it becomes less likely to win the approval of those for whom scholarship consists of a series of well-made, long-lasting bricks.

Although the obstinate humanity of the Greeks and Romans, and especially of their literature, made it impossible to banish personality and the role of the observer from scholarship, their manifestations can be kept at arm's length. In 1987 a well-known classicist began an essay on "The *Aeneid* as a Guide to Life" by distinguishing "scholarly under-

standing of the work" from "appreciation and values." "This subjectiv-
ity," he wrote, "generally should not be confused with scholarship,"
which he defined as nothing more than information about "the historical milieu, the society, the religion, the audience to which the work was
addressed at the time, and so on."[71] In the same year, the *American
Journal of Philology* proclaimed its editorial policy in terms that echoed
the same false dichotomy. It emphasized "rigorous scholarly methods,"
a preference that entailed the rejection of "articles on literary subjects
which are primarily appreciative" as well as "articles on philosophical
subjects which are primarily speculative."[72]

All this is a long way from Boeckh, for whom both criticism and
interpretation were equally essential parts of *Altertumswissenschaft*, a
long way from Nietzsche, and a long way as well from the Wilamowitz
who began his *History of Classical Scholarship* with an affirmation of the
resemblance between scholarship and mysticism:

> In this as in every department of knowledge — or to put it in the Greek
> way, in all philosophy — a feeling of wonder in the presence of some-
> thing we do not understand is the starting-point, the goal was pure,
> beatific contemplation of something we have come to understand in all
> its truth and beauty.[73]

The ghosts, Wilamowitz knew and Nietzsche might have agreed,
demand blood. But too many scholars in these times claim to practice
the *Altertumswissenschaft* of Wilamowitz without the moral engagement
that he knew was necessary before the ghosts would speak. A scholar,
he wrote, should be *vir bonus, discendi peritus* ("a good man, skilled at
learning").[74] As they perform their rituals and dream of the days when
Cargo came, our latter-day philologues, skilled though they are, sometimes fall as silent as the ghosts who refuse them speech.

Chapter 2

THE AMERICAN DIALECT

In 1936 Werner Jaeger, forty-eight years old, stood at the peak of a brilliant academic career. He was the author of a ground-breaking work on the development of Aristotle's thought and countless other books and articles; he held one of the most prestigious academic posts in the German-speaking world; he had founded *Die Antike*, a highbrow journal of classical culture read by Germany's movers and shakers; and two years earlier he had been invited to give the prestigious Sather Lectures at Berkeley. He enjoyed an international reputation and wielded public influence as well as academic power.

All these accomplishments weighed for nothing against the fact that Jaeger's second wife was a Jew. In 1936, it was time to leave the Third Reich. After a brief stopover at the University of Chicago, Jaeger accepted a university professorship created especially for him at Harvard. There he remained from 1939 until his death in 1961. At Harvard Jaeger taught quietly and effectively, influencing a generation of American classical scholars, and continued to publish important works of scholarship, but something had gone out of him. He never found anything like the public position, intellectual importance, or perhaps personal fulfillment that he had enjoyed in his native country.[1]

In his exile, Jaeger once remarked that without the prestige of Humanism, classical scholarship (*Altertumswissenschaft*) was a waste of time. Anyone who needed proof of this assertion, he went on to say, ought to come to America and learn from the way classical studies had developed there.[2] Jaeger recognized that in the New World old justifications for Classics no longer held, and that classical scholarship as he understood it needed roots in the society within which it was practiced. Like his teacher, Wilamowitz, he believed that *Altertumswissenschaft* treated questions that were important not merely to classical scholars, but also to society at large. Because the discourse of the governing classes in the European society that Jaeger knew had been shaped by continuous dialogue with classical antiquity, Jaeger saw the social and intellectual prestige of Greek and Roman antiquity as an essential context for classical scholarship.

As a young man, Jaeger had occupied the chair at Basel once held by Friedrich Nietzsche. Later he succeeded Wilamowitz in the chair of classical philology at the University of Berlin. In many important respects Jaeger sums up and synthesizes the quarrel between Nietzsche and Wilamowitz. Like Wilamowitz, he was deeply committed from his earliest manhood to the practice of the most rigorous and meticulous forms of *Altertumswissenschaft* and to the ideal of the study of antiquity as a whole. Like Nietzsche, he believed passionately that the proper understanding of the ancient world, and especially the ancient Greek world, could reform and revitalize modern life.[3] Yet in America, he found a new, strange world in which both the traditions inherited from *Altertumswissenschaft*'s greatest practitioner and the ideas of its most important critic failed to make sense.

Jaeger's experience in America is important and suggestive. Too often its lessons have been ignored by those who practice and think about Classics in this country. Classical studies is different in this New World. Liberal arts education and *Altertumswissenschaft* are not native growths, although one has been naturalized more successfully than the other. Newman, Wilamowitz, and Nietzsche, like other immigrants, had to drop their European ways and adapt to a new land and a new people. The European grammar of civility transformed itself into an American dialect of education.

LIBERAL ARTS IN AMERICA

In one sense classical education has been part of North America as long as the continent has known European settlement. Plans for schools and colleges on the familiar European pattern, with a curriculum centered on Latin and Greek, classical literature, and ancient history, appeared with the earliest colonists. In 1624 a certain Edward Palmer of London specified in his will that his American holdings could be used to found a university in Virginia, the Academia Virginiensis et Oxoniensis. The proposed institution was never built, but its name reveals Palmer's intention to establish an institution that would be a mirror site of Oxford in Virginia. Even earlier, in 1622, the Virginia Company had appointed a committee to examine a recently published book for its relevance to a proposed school for Indian and English children. The book was John Brinsley's *A Consolation for Our Grammar Schooles* (London: Richard Field, 1622), which argued that education in America—as well as in Ireland, Wales, Bermuda, and similar "ruder countries and places"—ought to be no different from that available in England.[4]

Brinsley's argument, and the need for it to be discussed in the New World, point to an important fact about classical studies in America. From the beginning, Classics has been a site of cultural tension. Thinking about classical studies has been a way to think about education and its place in a society in which nearly everything is negotiable.

The earliest settlers, especially in New England, saw education as part of their defense against a wilderness that was spiritually as well as physically dangerous. "We in this country," one Jonathan Mitchell wrote some twenty-five years after the founding of Harvard College, "being far removed from the more cultivated parts of the world, had need to use utmost care and diligence to keep up learning and all helps to education among us, lest degeneracy, barbarism, ignorance and irreligion do by degrees break in upon us."[5] In general, they responded to this danger by reproducing the familiar patterns of English education:

petty schools for instruction in the elements of literacy and numeracy, and where possible, grammar schools and universities to instruct an elite few in classical studies, theology, and mathematics. The famous Massachusetts School Act of November 11, 1647 (the "old deluder Satan" act) codified this pattern by prescribing that every town of fifty households was to establish a petty school, and every one with one hundred, a grammar school "to instruct youth so far as they may be fitted for the university."[6] Farther south, the pattern was little different. The regulations setting up the grammar school at the College of William and Mary specified classical education according to the English pattern:

> In this Grammar School let the Latin and Greek tongues be well taught. As for the Rudiments and Grammars, and Classick Authors of each tongue, let them teach the same Books which by Law or Custom are used in the Schools of England.[7]

By the next century, a classical curriculum based on the study of Latin and Greek and reading of ancient authors according to the familiar English pattern had been firmly established as the foundation and core of education for the relatively small number of young American men who hoped to become clergymen, statesmen, public servants, or teachers. It is important to remember how few ever reached the point of studying classical languages and their attendant subjects in a colonial college. Although many colleges were dreamed or even planned, only three actually operated in Britain's American colonies before 1740: Harvard, William and Mary, and Yale. Between 1642 and 1689, Harvard produced 388 graduates, nearly half of whom became clergymen. Massachusetts in 1689 had more than 48,000 inhabitants.[8] Classical studies in this country began as the education of an elite minority.

If there was ever a time in America when classical studies constituted the basis of the curriculum for all colleges and elite secondary schools, it was the century following 1640. In those years a small, largely clerical minority of Americans experienced an education based on the study of classical languages and the reading of classical authors.

Beginning in the second quarter of the eighteenth century, however, higher and elite secondary education underwent a transformation that marched in step with the change from colonial America to the independent United States. In this transformation classical education played an important role. By thinking about classical studies, Americans were able to sharpen the contours of debate on the merits of liberal as against practical education, on whether American education should be democratic or elitist, and on the kind of nation they hoped to build.

CLASSICS VS. PRACTICAL EDUCATION

In 1768 William Livingston responded to an Anglican bishop's criticism of the training of American clergy by reminding his lordship of what it was like to carve a new country from a wilderness:

> We want hands, my lord, more than heads. The most intimate acquaintance with the classics, will not remove our oaks; nor a taste for the *Georgics* cultivate our lands. Many of our young people are knocking their heads against the *Iliad*, who should employ their hands in clearing our swamps and draining our marshes. Others are musing, in cogitation profound, on the arrangement of a syllogism, while they ought to be guiding the tail of a plow.[9]

In the old country, John Locke had already found it "ridiculous . . . that a father should waste his own money, and his son's time, in setting him to learn the Roman language."[10] Locke himself drew on a distinctively English tradition, with its origin in the thought of Francis Bacon, in which knowledge was classified and valued according to where it came from and what it was good for. In this Baconian tradition, knowledge originating in experience had a higher value than knowledge drawn from books. Knowledge that led to practical uses had a higher value than knowledge that merely ornamented the character or established its possessor as a gentleman. In education as in so many other matters, the ideas of Locke and his tradition appealed to Americans newly aware of their separation from the traditions and elaborations of European culture.

Locke's followers exercised great influence over educational thought in eighteenth-century America. In 1720 John Clarke, the master of an English grammar school at Gloucester, published *An Essay upon the Education of Youth in Grammar Schools*. Clarke's treatise, according to Meyer Reinhold, served "as a *vade mecum* for teachers of Classics in America for generations."[11] Clarke advocated a mixed curriculum, in which Latin and Greek combined with "useful Knowledge" like history, ancient and modern geography, chronology, divinity, and English style. Two decades later America produced its own theory of mixed education. William Smith, a Scot who had immigrated to New York, produced *A General Idea of the College of Mirania* (1753). Smith's Miranians, after settling a new continent, have prospered to the point that they can set up an educational system for their utopia.

These young Miranians are shepherded into two groups, one destined to become clergymen, attorneys, physicians, and planters, and the other destined to become something else—engineers, mechanics, tradesmen, or businessmen. For three years the two groups receive the same education, in the hope that their friendships will mitigate class antagonism. Then their ways diverge. The second group goes off for a six-year course of training in English, arithmetic, and other practical arts, where they follow Locke's prescription to learn "writing a good hand, and casting accounts, which are of great advantage in all conditions of life, and to most trades indispensably necessary."[12] The first group has a longer task. Lawrence Cremin describes their course of study:

> Those destined for the learned professions proceed to a Latin school with a five-year program (four given over almost wholly to Latin with some minor studies in English and writing, and a fifth divided between Latin and Greek) and then to an undergraduate curriculum spanning four years—the first under a professor of mathematics, who teaches algebra, geometry, astronomy, chronology, and navigation along with such logic, metaphysics, and practical surveying as time and weather permit; the second under a professor of philosophy, who teaches ethics (out of Plato, Cicero, Locke, and Hutcheson), physics, natural history,

and mechanical and experimental philosophy; the third under a professor of rhetoric and poetry, who teaches the precepts of oratory and
the canons of taste and criticism (out of Cicero, Quintilian,
Demosthenes, and Aristotle); and the fourth under the direction of the
principal himself, who teaches agriculture and history, the former conceived as embracing hygiene, chemistry, and anatomy, and the latter
conceived as a series of lessons in ethics and politics.[13]

Smith's utopian ideas were not responsible for the way in which
American classical education differentiated itself from its English roots.
Intellectual history is not as simple as that. But Smith's *Mirania* did give
memorable expression to what was fast becoming a canonical distinction in American educational thought: on the one hand, liberal studies
whose distinctive character is that they are classical; on the other hand,
practical studies whose defining characteristic is that they are not classical. The debate over the merits of practical versus liberal education
became a debate about the merits and usefulness of classical studies.

Smith sent a copy of his book to Benjamin Franklin, who was
already deeply involved in the debate over useful education. In
Philadelphia the Quakers, following William Penn's condemnation of
Latin and Greek and praise of useful knowledge, advocated a "guarded
education" which emphasized religious instruction and vocational train-
ing at the expense, though not utter neglect, of Latin and Greek.[14]
Although Franklin was not himself a member of the Religious Society
of Friends, he admired some of their views and gave them expression in
his *Proposals Relating to the Education of the Youth in Pennsylvania* and
Constitutions of the Publick Academy in the City of Philadelphia (1749).[15]
In the "Advertisement to the Reader" introducing the *Proposals*
Franklin acknowledges other influences, giving pride of place to the
British tradition and to some of the same authors prescribed for the
advanced studies of Smith's Miranian classicists: Milton, Locke, and the
Scottish moral philosopher Francis Hutcheson.[16]

Franklin, as he recalled in a later memoir, had originally intended to
propose a school in which ancient languages would have no place, but
he was compelled to modify his intention under pressure from some

"persons of wealth and learning, whose subscriptions and countenance we should need."[17] In the 1749 *Proposals*, therefore, Franklin argued for an education that would combine classical and practical subjects. He wanted the youth of Pennsylvania to study "the dead and living languages, particularly their mother tongue," as well as "all useful branches of liberal arts and sciences."[18] In addition to Latin and Greek, his proposed curriculum included English, French, German, Spanish, history, geography, chronology, logic, rhetoric, writing, arithmetic, algebra, higher mathematics, natural and mechanic philosophy (i.e. science and engineering), and drawing.

In his *Proposals Relating to the Education of the Youth in Pennsylvania* Franklin emphasizes the practical, utilitarian value of education and gives classical, and indeed modern, languages only a limited place. He expresses the hope that when youth have reached an age to make a mature choice, they can be told about the utility and beauty of Latin and Greek and "thereby made desirous of learning these languages, and their industry sharpened in the acquisition of them."[19] Only then will divinity students be taught Latin and Greek; medical students Latin, Greek, and French; law students, Latin and French; and business students, modern languages. "Though all," he continues, "should not be compelled to learn Latin, Greek, or the modern foreign languages, yet none that have an ardent desire to learn them should be refused; their English, arithmetic, and other studies absolutely necessary being at the same time not neglected."

CLASSICS VS. DEMOCRATIC LIBERTY

Franklin's proposal, as he recalled forty years later, ran aground on the intractable prestige of classical education, which by 1750 had become naturalized in the elite grammar schools and colleges of the English colonies in the New World and in the minds of those educated in that tradition. Franklin had first proposed an "English school," with classical languages taught as an ancillary subject, if at all;[20] the *Constitutions of the Publick Academy in the City of Philadelphia*, which set out the actual plan of the new institution, records the first of many compromises in favor of elite, classical education. This document separates the "English School" from the "Latin School" and clearly establishes the priority of the latter department. The master of the Latin School is also to be rector of the whole academy; his salary is to be twice that of the English master, and he is to teach half as many students.

This decision, Franklin later remembered, reflected the priorities of an influential minority of the founding trustees:

> When the constitutions were first drawn, blanks were left for the salaries, and for the number of boys the Latin master was to teach. The first instance of partiality, in favor of the Latin part of the institution, was in giving the title of Rector to the Latin master, and no title to the English one. But the most striking instance was, when we met to sign, and the blanks were first to be filled up, the votes of a majority carried it to give twice as much salary to the Latin master as to the English, and yet require twice as much duty from the English master as from the Latin. . . . However, the Trustees who voted these salaries being themselves by far the greatest subscribers, though not the most numerous, it was thought they had a kind of right to predominate in money matters; and those, who had wished an equal regard might have been shown to both schools, submitted, though not without regret, and at times some little complaining. . . .[21]

The arrangements that vexed Franklin appear to have been usual in institutions divided between "Latin schools" and "English schools." According to a report made in 1784 by a committee of the Quaker monthly meeting in Philadelphia, the master of their Latin school received a regular salary as well as an allowance for an "usher" or assistant teacher, while the master of the English school, who taught eighty-eight boys as opposed to the Latin master's thirty, seems to have depended on his students' fees and to have done without an usher.[22] The regulations drawn up for The Episcopal Academy in Philadelphia at its founding in 1785 established Latin, English, and mathematical schools but made the master of the Latin school headmaster. Franklin's vexation was prompted not only by his commitment to utilitarian education, but also by his sense that the preference given to classical education reflected its association with power and wealth.

After Americans threw off the tyranny of Great Britain, they looked around for new tyrants to reject. Greek and Latin offered themselves, and in the early Federal period the comparison between the place of ancient languages in education and tyranny became almost a commonplace. The *Massachusetts Magazine* of December 1789, published excerpts from a letter sent by Hugh Williamson, M.D., to William Samuel Johnson, the president of Columbia College in New York. Classical education, Dr. Williamson wrote, amounted to "grievous servitude" under what he called "the tyranny of Greek and Latin."[23] Also in 1789, Benjamin Rush wrote of the need to combat "this formidable enemy of human reason . . . this tyrant."[24] Two years later, in his *Plan for the General Establishment of Schools Throughout the United States* (1791), Robert Coram declared the connection between independence from foreign influence, religious and personal liberty, and an education free of Latin and Greek: "no modes of faith, systems of manners, or foreign or dead languages should be taught in these schools. As none of them are necessary to obtain a knowledge of the obligations of society, the government is not bound to instruct the citizens in anything of the kind."[25]

In the new nation, classical studies could easily be seen as representing everything that the Revolution had cast off: ancient privilege, tyranny, and the elitism of power and wealth. By casting classical languages out of education in the name of utilitarianism and democracy, nationalist reformers declared educational independence from the Old World and asserted the superiority of the New. "I have no notion," Thomas Paine wrote, "of yielding the palm of the United States to any Grecians and Romans that were ever born."[26]

CLASSICS VS. THE NEW NATION

Classical languages and classical knowledge were not, of course, cast out of American political and cultural life, despite the best efforts of Rush, Paine, and other radical reformers. During the Revolutionary and early Federal periods, in fact, classical influences dominated American political life and cultural expression. The idea of our nation grew out of a dialogue between the Founders and the ancient world, and from the columns in our Capitol to the Latin on our currency, superficial signs of their engagement with Greek and Roman antiquity are everywhere. That engagement with antiquity, like the larger Enlightenment project of which it forms a part, was not simple emulation or ornamental erudition.[27] Those classical columns do actually hold up something in the thought of Jefferson, Adams, and the other Founders.

It is difficult, in fact, to point to any more profound students of classical thought and literature in late eighteenth-century America than Jefferson and Adams. Their correspondence may be the most perceptive work of classical scholarship produced in North America between the first draft of Sandys's translation of Ovid's *Metamorphoses* and Gildersleeve's edition of Pindar, and published works like Adams's *Defence of the Constitutions of the United States* teem with intensive, perceptive analysis of Greek and Roman political systems.[28] No distinction in education or practice separated professional classicists—if that is the right word for the men who made their living as schoolmasters and college tutors—from the governing elite of Revolutionary America. The Enlightenment's dialogue with classical antiquity touched some more deeply than others but left none unaffected.

The story of classical influences on America's founding ideology is well known, in part because generations of classicists anxious to claim or justify a position in national life and education have promoted and retold it. The rejection of classical education entirely by numerous influential thinkers in the same founding period is less often recalled. Substantial numbers of thinking people, then as now, regarded the Classics with deep suspicion. Benjamin Rush wrote to John Adams on June 15, 1789, "I shall class them [Greek and Latin] hereafter with Negro slavery and spiritous liquors, and consider them as, though in a less degree, unfriendly to the progress of morals, knowledge, and religion in the United States."[29] Rush's proposal for a federal university, which appeared in the Philadelphia *Federal Gazette* for October 29, 1788, made no provision for the study of Greek and Latin. Rejection of the Classics, Rush hoped, would distinguish the vigorous, practical curriculum of the federal university from the effete, quisquilian studies of its European counterparts:

> While the business of education in Europe consists in lectures upon the ruins of Palmyra and the antiquities of Herculaneum, or in disputes about Hebrew points, Greek particles, or the accent and quantity of the Roman language, the youth of America will be employed in acquiring those branches of knowledge which increase the conveniences of life, lessen human misery, improve our country, promote population, exalt the human understanding, and establish domestic, social, and political happiness.[30]

Classical studies endure, however, though not in the form against which Rush inveighed. Franklin's struggle to establish a utilitarian curriculum for the Academy and College of Philadelphia, and the elitist-dominated compromise that resulted there and elsewhere, typify the accommodation reached in a nation with a knack for just that kind of compromise between innovation and continuity. They demonstrate, also, the way in which classical studies served as a focal point for a complex set of related arguments over useful knowledge, democratic education, and the best course of action for the new nation. Those who shared agreement with one side or another on any one of these issues were likely also to share views on the others. Classics in the 1790s played much the same role in the debates of the American governing class that literary theory or multiculturalism played in the discourse of academics in the 1990s. It provided a clear ground for debate, and by discussing classical studies, it was possible to imply one's position in the dialectic from which the new nation was being born.

After the momentous questions of independence and the organization of the new federal polity had been settled, Classics receded from the public arena. Americans began to look at the classical past with different eyes. Ancient precedent, which had been so useful as they thought about forming a new nation, now seemed less relevant. "So different was the style of society then, and with those people," the aged Jefferson wrote in 1816, "from what it is now and with us, that I think little edification can be obtained from their writings on the subject of government."[31] In the first three decades of the nineteenth century, debating the role of classical studies became a means of giving voice to a number of related anxieties that grew out of the national act of self-definition. As they thought about education and scholarship, the Americans whom Alexis de Tocqueville observed came increasingly to think of themselves as an unclassical people.

In this process classical studies acquired the character that so perplexed Werner Jaeger a century later. During the years between President Jefferson and President Jackson, American classical studies developed the sense, which persisted into the late twentieth century, of identification with and abiding inferiority to its European model, and by the end of that period its alienation from American public life prefigured the later marginal role of the humanities in general.

American education had from its beginnings imitated the forms and values of education in the British homeland, and at its higher, elite levels had imported that system's emphasis on classical studies and in particular on the study of classical languages. Despite calls for change from radical Humanist reformers like Isaac Comenius or moderates like Roger Ascham, instruction in Latin and Greek followed for the most part a pattern unchanged since the Renaissance. Boys (mostly) memorized the elements of language, grammatical rules and lexical items, and then applied them to increasingly difficult texts. Reading meant deciphering texts according to a highly elaborate, coded construction of the language in which they were written, and schooling became a series of ritualized exercises in memorizing that code. Failure to commit the code to memory or to decipher accurately was penalized by beating, and the bundle of birch rods used for these floggings became the most potent symbol of educational authority.[32]

This system of code, ritual, reward, and punishment applied to young males gathered around it all the mystery and power of a rite of passage from boyhood to manhood.[33] When it was transported to the New World, it became in addition the locus of anxieties about the success of the new nation's declaration of independence from the fatherland and the old king. It exaggerates only a little to see psychological processes and profound struggles of identity at the heart of the debate over the role of classical studies in the new United States. Benjamin West passionately conveys his sense of the cruelty of the process that confined boys like prisoners or insects and condemned them to a foolish task: "There is no play common among children that strikes me with an idea of half the folly that I am struck with every time I look into a Latin school and see thirty or forty boys pinioned down to benches and declining nouns, conjugating verbs, or writing Latin versions."[34] The scene "strikes" West, and he emphasizes the verb by repetition, just as blow after blow emphasized and punctuated the experience of young males in the Latin schools.

When Americans compared themselves to their British and European progenitors, they naturally looked to classical education as a measuring rod. In the first uncertain decades of nationhood, they often seemed to fall short. Both supporters of classical education and critics like West acknowledged this deficiency with concern. Even at Yale, according to a member of the class of 1826, the instructors were merely "good drill masters." Everywhere Americans looked, they saw their classical education deficient in comparison with that of Britain or Europe. The *Analectic Magazine* in 1813 found American classical studies "at the lowest ebb," and a plethora of "seminaries of learning of the highest pretensions," many of which, "invested with all the powers and dignities of colleges, will not bear a comparison with the grammar-schools of England, or the second grade of French schools."[35] In 1819 Joseph Green Cogswell compared American academies "in all that relates to classical learning" to Prussian secondary schools, including the academy that would later educate Wilamowitz and Nietzsche: "there is not one, from Maine to Georgia, which has yet sent forth a single first rate scholar; no, not one since the settlement of the country, equal even to the most ordinary of the thirty or forty, which come out every year from Schule Pforta, and Meissen."[36]

These plaints spawned a litany of depreciation that continued into the age of e-mail.[37] Like their progeny, they reflect a deeper insecurity and a larger problem than simply the perceived inferiority of American to European classical education. By the time Cogswell made his comparison, Classics had moved from the center of American educational life to the periphery. That is where Alexis de Tocqueville found it when he and his comrade Gustave de Beaumont visited America in 1831–1832.

One evening the two young men approached a cabin somewhere on the frontier. The hearth flame could be seen flickering through the chinks in the wall, and the roof of boughs shook in the wind. In Europe, Tocqueville reflected, a similar dwelling in a similar forest would shelter a person living in want and ignorance, whose life had changed little since the days of the Roman Empire. The European peasant seemed a fit inhabitant for his rude hut, and an unbridgeable gulf separated him from the civilization of cities and towns.

In America, on the other hand, even the word "peasant" was unknown. Instead, the cabin in the backwoods sheltered a different kind of human being altogether, one called a pioneer:

> Everything about him is primitive and wild, but he is himself the result
> of the labor and experience of eighteen centuries. He wears the dress
> and speaks the language of cities; he is acquainted with the past, curi-
> ous about the future, and ready for argument about the present; he is,
> in short, a highly civilized being, who consents for a time to inhabit the
> backwoods, and who penetrates into the wilds of the New World with
> the Bible, an axe, and some newspapers.[38]

This pioneer is civilized, but with the possible exception of the Bible, classical literature plays no part in his civility. His education has not produced a scholar as Cogswell understood it; in America, in fact, learned men are few, and ignorant men almost unknown. American education, as far as Tocqueville could observe, aimed at producing a population situated between the extremes of learning and ignorance.

Tocqueville's *Democracy in America* preserves, almost as if in amber, a crucial moment in American culture. Tocqueville may have been the first European to pay attention to Americans as a distinct people. He may also have been among the first Europeans who could. In 1800 we were Englishmen in the forest. In 1830 we were a new kind of political, social, and cultural animal, and even in the late twentieth century, an American reader of Tocqueville experiences a shock of recognition. There we are.

Tocqueville found a new and unclassical world. Americans, he discovered, should never be led to talk of Europe, for that topic brought on all the "presumption and very foolish pride" of people well-informed about their own nation and ignorant of others.[39] He does not, however, seem to have found the sense of inferiority in the face of European classical learning expressed by Joseph Green Cogswell in 1819. None of Tocqueville's moderately learned pioneers laid down axe, Bible, and newspapers to lament that he did not know Latin and Greek as well as the boys of Westminster or Pforte.

Tocqueville's Americans, in fact, are the first for whom classical studies held only a marginal place in cultural and intellectual life. Six years after Tocqueville's visit, an audience of those Americans gathered on the last day of August at one of their ancient institutions of learning, already two centuries old, to hear Ralph Waldo Emerson deliver an address celebrating the beginning of the academic year. According to Oliver Wendell Holmes, who was among them, the audience at Harvard divided along generational lines. Senior professors and clergymen did not know what to make of Emerson's remarks, "but the young men went out from it as if a prophet had been proclaiming to them, 'Thus saith the Lord.' No listener ever forgot that address," which Holmes calls "our intellectual Declaration of Independence."[40]

Emerson's "The American Scholar" outlines a new vision of the life of the mind. Its influence on American education was profound. It hardly mentions Greece, Rome, or classical studies. Emerson proclaims instead a radical individualism for a nation whose scholars unite with their fellow citizens in a union of hand and heart unlike any that has existed in other nations:

> We will walk on our own feet; we will work with our own hands; we will speak our own minds. The study of letters shall be no longer a name for pity, for doubt, and for sensual indulgence. The dread of man and the love of man shall be a wall of defense and a wreath of joy around all. A nation of men will for the first time exist, because each believes himself inspired by the Divine Soul which also inspires all men.[41]

In a passage that seems especially to have troubled the older and more conservative members of his audience,[42] Emerson rejects the grand, classical, and medieval cultures of the Old World—Italy, Greece, Arabia, and Provence—in favor of "the meal in the firkin; the milk in the pan; the ballad in the street; the news of the boat; the glance of the eye; the form and gait of the body."[43] Here, as often, Emerson anticipates Whitman. In the primary world of everyday reality and not in the derived world of languages and texts, his American scholar will find material.

Unlike Newman, who felt no need to make the obvious specification that by "grammar" or "literary studies" he meant the grammar of Latin and Greek and studies in the literature of those languages, Emerson deliberately excludes or de-emphasizes the traditional, classical foundations of education. Three influences produce his ideal American scholar: Nature, which he identifies with the Transcendentalist universal Mind; the mind of the Past; and Experience or Action. Only the mind of the Past presents dangers to be avoided. Emerson represents these dangers by indirect allusion to the philological criticism of texts that stood at the center of traditional, European classical studies:

> Hence, instead of Man Thinking, we have the bookworm. Hence the book-learned class, who value books, as such; not as related to nature and the human constitution, but as making a sort of Third Estate with the world and the soul. Hence the restorers of readings, the emendators, the bibliomaniacs of all degrees.[44]

Emerson knew what *Altertumswissenschaft* was. He had developed his image of it fifteen years earlier when his brother William, who was a student at the Göttingen of Wolf and Eichhorn, had reported at length from what young Ralph called a "paradise of dictionaries and critics."[45]

"The American Scholar" was, as Holmes saw, prophetic, although like many prophecies, it came true in a way that contradicted its prophet's hopes. Emerson hoped for an unclassical, American scholarship that would be engaged with American life, and for colleges that would "aim not to drill, but to create," that would "set the hearts of their youth on flame."[46] Instead he defined the alienation of classical, liberal arts education from the American life of action. Emerson wanted his American scholar to be free and brave, not a sheltered recluse: "It is a shame to him if his tranquility, amid dangerous times, arise from the presumption that like children and women his is a protected class; or if he seek a temporary peace by the diversion of his thoughts from politics or vexed questions, hiding his head like an ostrich in the flowering bushes, peeping into microscopes, and turning rhymes, as a boy whistles to keep his courage up."[47] Ten years before Emerson spoke at Harvard, a typically American educational compromise had made it inevitable that his worst fears, and not his transcendental hopes, would come true.

CLASSICS UNDER ATTACK: THE OLD COLLEGE AND THE MOVE TOWARD THE AMERICAN UNIVERSITY

In 1833 another audience had gathered at Harvard to witness the presentation of an honorary doctorate to President Andrew Jackson. The degree ceremony was, of course, conducted in Latin, and Josiah Quincy, the president of Harvard, delivered an address in the same language. The time came for President Jackson to respond in the universal language of learned men. Years later Dr. Quincy's son, who had served as aide to Jackson on the occasion, recalled the popular belief that the general had delivered the following memorable oration, which gathered all the Latin he knew: "Ex post facto; e pluribus unum; sic semper tyrannis; quid pro quo." In fact Jackson "mumbled something in the vernacular which nobody heard."[48] The story was too good not to be told, however, and it appears in more than one version. The point of it, contemporary witnesses agreed, was not to mock the unlearned frontiersman whose reading was in fact almost limited to the Bible and newspapers.[49] It showed rather, Dr. Quincy's son suggested, that "a man of the people could triumph over the crafts and subtleties" of Latin-speaking elitists.[50]

Jackson's short speech and Emerson's longer one mark the new place of classical studies in American life. As long as the new nation worked to define itself in the Revolutionary and early Federal era, the dialectic opposition of classical studies and democracy ensured that Classics occupied a central place in our national conversation. In Jacksonian America, however, Classics moved from the arena of political life into the academic world of schools and universities. The more Americans developed a sense of themselves as a people unique in history, the more classical precedents seemed irrelevant to decisions about public life.

Even in the academy, the new nation's growing consciousness of its political and psychological independence from the culture of its European founders led to a gradual repositioning of the role of classical studies, both in the older schools and colleges and in the new institutions founded as the nation expanded westward. Classical studies increasingly moved to the margins of developing American academic life — not, however, without a struggle.

In Jackson's and Emerson's America, the humanistic, classical liberal arts, which had been transplanted into the colonies' earliest grammar schools and colleges, endured in attenuated form as part of the curriculum in what Gerald Graff and others have called the Old College. This convenient term embraces some of the prevolutionary foundations, like Yale, Columbia, and Princeton (known as "The College of New Jersey" until 1860), as well as Amherst, Bowdoin, Dickinson, Middlebury, Williams, and many other small institutions founded by Christian denominations for the fundamental purpose of training ministers. In these institutions all students followed a uniform course of study through four years. The study of Greek and Latin authors and ancient history formed a substantial part of this curriculum, especially in the first two years. In 1830 Henry Vethlake, a critic of this curriculum, offered a concise description:

> The students of our colleges, it is well known, are almost universally divided into four different classes, viz: the Freshman, Sophomore, Junior, and Senior Classes. The course of study in each of them endures for a year, and is the same for every student, whatever may be his capacity or tastes. A candidate for admission to the Freshman or lowest class, besides possessing a competent knowledge of various branches of what is usually styled an *English* education, such as English Grammar, Geography, &c. must come prepared to be examined on a certain number, or on portions of a certain number of the classical (Greek and Latin) authors; and the Greek and Latin languages are also usually the principal subjects of study during the first two years of the collegiate course, the sciences only becoming predominant objects of the students' attention in the Junior and Senior years.[51]

The Old College's curriculum, with its content founded on Latin and Greek, its uniform course of study, and its often sectarian purpose, was not the only pattern for higher education in the emerging nation. William Livingston's plea for an education that would guide the hands of citizens of the New World found realization in plans for new kinds of educational institutions and in a debate over the purpose and nature of American higher education that reverberated over the generations between Jackson's presidency and the Civil War.

Thomas Jefferson's plans for the University of Virginia grew out of discussions among the founding generation of the new republic. George Washington had argued strongly for a national university that would bring together students from all parts of the country, alleviate sectional divisions, and educate leaders for the new polity. Benjamin Rush's "Plan of a Federal University" would be a postgraduate institution, accepting only students who had earned a degree from colleges in their own states. Rush's curriculum emphasized studies that would prepare men to govern the new nation and advance its prosperity: history, law, agriculture, engineering, and military science. There was no room in Rush's plan, or in Rush's United States, for traditional classical studies.

Jefferson was better disposed toward Classics. The Rockfish Gap report of 1818, which laid out the basic plan for the new University of Virginia, was the work of a committee of twenty-one Virginians headed by Jefferson. The committee proposed ten schools, each headed by a professor. Ancient languages (Latin, Greek, and Hebrew) were to be the work of one of these schools, but the main weight of the curriculum was concentrated in modern studies: European languages, pure mathematics, "physico-mathematics" (physics, astronomy, and geography), natural philosophy (chemistry, agriculture, and mineralogy), botany and zoology, anatomy and medicine, political science, civil law, and "ideology" (philosophy, grammar, ethics, rhetoric, belles-lettres, and fine arts).

The real revolution in Jefferson's curriculum, however, lay not in the subjects studied but in how the student approached them. The Old College curriculum had been just that: a single course of study in which all students encountered the same subjects, in the same order, for four years, in a sequence moving from basic literary and historical texts to moral philosophy and theology. This sequence mirrored to some extent the sequence of faculties in the medieval university, from arts through civil and canon law to divinity, and assumed that subjects could be arranged in hierarchical order, culminating in moral philosophy and theology. Jefferson's curriculum, on the other hand, was actually multiple curricula, separate courses of study that could be pursued in any order, without any but the most elementary prerequisites. "We shall," Jefferson wrote, "allow [the students] uncontrolled choice in the lectures they shall choose to attend, and require elementary qualifications only, and sufficient age."[52]

In this system a structured classical education originally designed for a European governing class and modified for the professional classes of a republic was replaced by a democratic, libertarian program of choices intended to form, as the Rockfish Gap report put it, "the statesmen, legislators & judges, on whom public prosperity & individual hap-

piness are so much to depend." In this program classical studies constituted only one possibility among many courses of study, and it lost the
foundational position it held in the Old College's structured curriculum.
Jefferson himself believed that a single year of study would be enough
to give a student's classical studies a "last polish."[53]

Jefferson's design for the University of Virginia was not the first to
reject the Old College's structured classical education in favor of a program of education for scientific achievements, practical knowledge, and
political liberty. There had been earlier experiments at the College of
Philadelphia (later the University of Pennsylvania) and at Harvard, and
in 1817, as the Rockfish Gap committee was finishing its report,
Augustus B. Woodward proposed a plan for a university in Michigan
whose name, "Catholicoepistemiad," revealed his intention that it be an
institution embracing the whole range of human knowledge. Jefferson's
design, however, was the most rigorously argued and coherently
designed anticlassical program of the new republic and the first to
translate such a coherent design into a functioning institution supported
by public resources. Jefferson's curriculum promised to answer the new
country's need for "hands . . . more than heads," as William Livingston
had noted even before the Revolution (above, p. 47), and it satisfied the
American desire that education be useful, which had grown from the
soil of Locke's ideas on education.

For a time, it appeared that the Jeffersonian model would prevail
and that classical studies in the new nation's universities would be not
the ground of education but one subject among many, and that not the
most important. In fact, for half a century between the founding of the
University of Virginia and the Civil War, debate raged over what an
American institution of higher education should look like, whether it
should follow Jefferson's pattern or continue with the classical, uniform
education of the Old College. Even though the ambitious plan of the
Rockfish Gap committee underwent several modifications in the face of
financial reality, it remained a touchstone for one side of the controversy. For the other side, another committee report fortified the ground
that the Old College would defend to its death.

On September 11, 1827, the president and fellows of Yale College resolved to appoint a high-powered committee, consisting of the governor of Connecticut, the president of Yale, and three other distinguished gentlemen, "to inquire into the expediency of so altering the regular course of instruction in this college, as to leave out of said course the study of the *dead languages*, substituting other studies therefor; and either requiring a competent knowledge of said languages, as a condition of admittance into the college, or providing instruction in the same, for such as shall choose to study them after admittance."[54] Yale, in other words, was to consider following the pattern of Jefferson's university and other modern, American institutions. Classical studies, the Latin and Greek languages, would cease to be the principal subject of the first years of a uniform college course and the ground of education in the rest and would become one option among many.

A year later the committee produced what has been called "the most influential document in American higher education in the first half of the nineteenth century."[55] The Yale Report of 1828 defends what it calls "literary education," by which it means the classically based curriculum of the Old College. It acknowledges that this curriculum is not exactly the same as its European ancestor, the Renaissance classical education criticized by Locke, but it does not presume to condemn "every feature, in systems of instruction which have had an origin more ancient than our republican seminaries."[56] President Day and his colleagues justify, in terms that are sometimes surprisingly reminiscent of modern apologies for liberal arts education, a plan of education that develops mental abilities, excludes strictly professional studies but prepares students to learn any profession, and includes essential elements of contemporary culture as well as the best of the past. It is easy to see why Richard Lanham sees a strong resemblance between the Yale Report and the arguments of Edward Hirsch, William Bennett, and other modern proponents of traditional liberal education.[57]

But the general argument in favor of what looks almost like modern liberal education is only half of the Yale Report of 1828. The Yale committee had been charged, after all, with investigating whether it would be a good idea to eliminate instruction in Latin and Greek and replace it with other subjects; as the authors of the report made clear, the section dealing with the general character of collegiate education was only a preface to the defense of the classical languages:

> The expediency of retaining the ancient languages, as an essential part of our course of instruction, is so obviously connected with the object and plan of education in the college, that justice could not be done to the particular subject of inquiry in the resolution, without a brief statement of the nature and arrangement of the various branches of the whole system. The report of the faculty was accordingly made out in *two parts*; one containing a summary view of the plan of education in the college; the other, an inquiry into the expediency of insisting on the study of the ancient languages.[58]

Just as modern readers often fail to see that when Newman talks about "grammar" and "liberal education," he means Latin grammar and classical education, so modern readers of the Yale Report often overlook the fact that it is not talking about the kind of education provided in modern liberal arts colleges or defended by Hirsch, Bennett, and other modern apologists. President Day and his colleagues were clear in their thinking: liberal education, or as they usually called it, "literary education," meant a fundamentally classical education, grounded in the study of Latin and Greek and aware of its continuity with the humanistic classical education of the Renaissance. The ancient languages were "an essential part" of the curriculum, and it was impossible to discuss the "plan of education" at Yale and similar institutions without thinking about them.

The Yale committee of 1828 put forward three arguments in favor of keeping classical languages in their traditional place at the center of the curriculum: an argument from value, an argument from psychology, and an argument from utility. All of them are products of their time and place; although they are flawed, none of them is entirely unworthy of consideration today, and in some form they can still be found in the arguments of apologists for the Classics.

First, the committee argued that knowledge of classical literature was both necessary and valuable: necessary to understand allusions in literature, art, and educated conversation, and valuable "on the ground of its distinct and independent merits. Familiarity with the Greek and Roman writers is especially adapted," they wrote, "to form the taste, and to discipline the mind, both in thought and diction, to the relish of what is elevated, chaste, and simple."[59] In a less assertive form, something like this argument figures in modern debates over the canon of the humanities, usually in the form of conservative insistence on the unique relevance and value of classical literature, broadly understood — Shakespeare as well as Sophocles — and on its superiority to the transient or unproved work of nondead, nonwhite, nonmale authors.

It is, then, worth noting that the authors of the Yale Report made claims that were of their time and place, and so less imperially prescriptive than those of Lynne Cheney, William Bennett, or Edward Hirsch. The committee in New Haven acknowledged that part at least of its case for classical learning depended on "the present state of the world" and on the need for communication among an educated, international elite in America and Europe. They approached this elite as educators of a new nation, conscious of the risk that they might appear as raw frontiersmen in the face of European cultural superiority:

> Whoever . . . without a preparation in classical literature, engages in any literary investigation, or undertakes to discuss any literary topic, or associates with those who in any country of Europe, or in this country, are acknowledged to be men of liberal acquirements, immediately feels a deficiency in his education, and is convinced that he is destitute of an important part of practical learning. If scholars, then, are to be prepared to act in the literary world as it in fact exists, classical literature, from considerations purely practical, should form an important part of their early discipline.[60]

These American academics from 1828 are not progenitors of Cheney and Bennett, or even of modern teachers of Classics at places like Yale, but of those who work to bring students from historically excluded groups into the great conversation that the West has always held with Greece and Rome.[61]

Second, the committee made an argument based in part on faculty psychology, the belief that the mind has distinct faculties or powers, each of which operates independently and can be separately developed. Faculty psychology is no longer generally accepted, although something like it, the theory of multiple intelligences, now enjoys a vogue among educationists. To the authors of the Yale Report, the fact that classical study "forms the most effectual discipline of the mental faculties" seemed so obvious as hardly to need mentioning, and they allowed their discussion to elide into a rather different issue: the ability of classical studies to serve as a complete education, not only for an individual as his mental faculties develop, but also for many different kinds of people with diverse abilities:

> It must be obvious to the most cursory observer, that the classics afford materials to exercise talent of every degree, from the first open-ing of the youthful intellect to the period of its highest maturity. The range of classical study extends from the elements of language, to the most difficult questions arising from literary research and criticism.[62]

This argument remains one of the best in favor of the deep, lifelong study of Classics, and it does not depend on a belief in faculty psychol-ogy. It is one that cannot be made in the context either of the Jeffersonian university or of the modern disciplinary institution, because it is an argument about classical education, not about Classics as a separate subject or academic discipline. If, the Yale Report's authors knew, a person spends a lifetime, from childhood to adulthood, studying classical languages and the civilizations they encode, there is a chance that that person will be an educated human being. It is hard to think of another one of the humanities of which this can be said.

Faculty psychology, in fact, and the related idea of education as mental discipline, remained very much alive in American educational thought through the nineteenth century. As the modern university developed in the years following the Civil War, small colleges clung to it as one of their justifications for an education that was neither research-oriented nor aimed at any specific profession or career. In time, the idea of mental discipline became one of the bases from which developed the American idea of liberal education.[63]

Finally, the committee put forward an argument that can only seem quaint. Classics, they maintained, forms the most practical preprofessional training available, especially for divinity, law, and medicine. In words that foreshadow the courses in etymology, vocabulary building, and scientific terminology that pack in students and pay the bills for many Classics departments in modern American universities, the committee emphasizes the connection between classical languages and medical terminology:

> In the profession of medicine, the knowledge of the Greek and Latin languages is less necessary now than formerly; but even at the present time it may be doubted, whether the facilities which classical learning affords for understanding and rendering familiar the terms of science, do not more than counterbalance the time and labor required for obtaining this learning.[64]

Even in the context of 1828, this has the air of a counsel of desperation. (It may be worth pointing out, though, that in the early nineteenth century some physicians, at least, could be expected to work in ancient languages; the only nearly complete edition in Greek of the works of the second-century physician Galen, Thomas Kühn's of 1834, has an index that is directed toward practicing physicians, not classical philologists.)

The Yale Report of 1828 often receives credit, or in some quarters blame, for ensuring that something like traditional classical education remained the norm in American colleges until after the Civil War. Its defense of liberal education, and of education as training for the mind rather than preparation for a profession, certainly laid part of the groundwork for that characteristically American institution, the small liberal arts college, and in its soil Newman's transplanted idea of a university took root and flourished. The Yale Report's traditionalism contrasts with Jefferson's Lockean pragmatism in the Rockfish Gap report; one committee's work points the way to Amherst, Williams, and Swarthmore; the other to Columbia, Michigan, and Berkeley.

This dichotomous scheme may serve as a rough guide to the origins of American higher education's two most characteristic institutional forms. It will not account for what happened to classical studies in American higher education during the mid-nineteenth century. Despite their apparent contrast in ideology and institutional progeny, both the Jeffersonian university and the Old College in the wake of the Yale Report became institutional configurations in which there was less and less room for classical studies. In the Jeffersonian university this was a matter of design: in seeking to create an education for their new country and to make room for subjects that seemed urgent and important, Jefferson and like-minded pragmatists deliberately moved the study of Greek and Latin from the center of the curriculum to the periphery. In the case of the Old College, it exaggerates only a little to say that the Yale Report's rhetorical strategy succeeded only too well.

President Day and his colleagues had been asked to defend the study of classical languages and literature in the context of Yale College's curriculum. The Classics, they felt, needed no defense; as they said in presenting the connection between study of the Classics and development of mental faculties, "This is a topic so often insisted on, that little need be said of it here."[65] The long history of classical education and its universal identification with the kind of education that they were defending seemed to indicate that they could relegate classical studies to the second part of their report. They could appeal to "the general estimation in which it is held in the literary world, and its intrinsic merits,"[66] in the confidence that their readers would agree. Their main energy went toward defending their college and its curriculum and justifying a particular kind of education. That, for them, was what classical education was: literary and liberal education, which would allow those who possessed it to enter into the community of an educated elite not only in America, but in Europe as well. No Yale graduate would, they hoped, be a person who, "without a preparation in classical literature, engages in any literary investigation, or undertakes to discuss any literary topic, or associates with those who in any country of Europe, or in this country, are acknowledged to be men of liberal acquirements."[67] If anything, Yale needed more classical studies, not less: "From the graduates of this college, who have visited Europe, complaints have sometimes been heard, that their classical attainments were too small for the literature of the old world; but none are recollected to have expressed regret, that they had cultivated ancient learning while here, however much time they might have devoted to this subject."[68]

In the America of 1828, however, classical studies, not the general concept of literary and liberal education, needed defending. The apparent strength of the Greek and Latin foundations of education at Yale and similar institutions was an illusion. They were already crumbling, because they were unsupported by anything in the culture and society that their advocates claimed they served. On his visit to America two years after the Yale Report, Tocqueville found citizens of a democracy unlike any polity in Europe. These independent citizens were already forging a new culture in which classical humanism played little part in civic culture.

Americans in New York and Philadelphia, Richmond and Charleston were, of course, building capitols, banks, and schools with columns, giving their new towns names ending in -opolis, -opia, and -oria, and naming their slaves Cassius or Ganymede. But these signs of classicism do not make the America of the 1830s, 1840s, and 1850s a classical civilization. The success of our revolution, the durability of its consequences, and the eminent rationality of its planners obscure its radicalism. As they debated classical precedents and patterns for the new republic, the Founders did away with the conditions that might have allowed the Old World's classical humanism to move to the New. Humanistic classical education depended on the existence of the class it had been designed to serve, and that aristocratic, leisured class, governing well or badly but always by right, had no place in the new nation of Tocqueville's pioneers. Nor did the education intended to form that class's tastes, values, and attitudes.

More than any other, Thomas Jefferson, the careful student of Plutarch and Livy, the builder of Palladian Monticello, bears responsibility for the failure of classical humanism to transplant itself to America. The self-evident truths of the Declaration of Independence, for all their complex roots in a Greco-Roman tradition of thought about individuality, liberty, and the aims of human life, directly contradict the premises of classical humanism. The nation's long struggle, in its first century of existence and since, to accept and enact Jefferson's truths can be seen as a struggle to become something other than a society derived from the humanist attempt to reinvent classical antiquity—to become, as Jefferson's best exegete put it, "a new nation, conceived in liberty and dedicated to the proposition that all men are created equal."[69]

In the course of this struggle, classical studies in American colleges and universities moved into the margins of the curriculum. The Old College, with its curriculum based on classical languages, found it harder and harder to attract students to its uniform course of study. Many students found alternative ways to prepare for the learned professions of law, medicine, and theology, and the colleges began to lose even their traditional clientele. Prompted as much by diminishing enrollments and declining revenue as by a sense of their own declining importance to American society, the colleges debated reform. None of the proposed solutions increased, or even maintained, the place of Classics at the heart of the curriculum.

In 1850 Brown University's president, Francis Wayland, reported to the Brown Corporation on a proposal to reform the curriculum by liberalizing entrance requirements, introducing new subjects, and allowing students to choose, within limits, what course of study they would follow. President Wayland was under no illusions about the effect of his proposals on the foundations of Brown's traditional curriculum:

> The objection that would arise to this plan, would probably be its effect upon the classics. It will be said, that we should thus diminish the amount of study bestowed on Latin and Greek. To this the reply is easy. If, by placing Latin and Greek upon their own merits, they are

unable to retain their present place in the education of civilized and Christianized man, then let them give place to something better. They have, by right, no preeminence over other studies, and it is absurd to claim it for them.

Wayland assumes what he could hardly deny, that his proposals would in fact lead to a decline in the amount of time available for and devoted to classical languages. He did not regard this as a loss; in his view, which many of his contemporaries shared, time spent on Latin and Greek was time wasted:

> In our present system we devote some six or seven years to the compulsory study of the classics. Besides innumerable academies, we have one hundred and twenty colleges, in which, for a large part of the time, classical studies occupy the labors of the student. And what is the fruit? How many of these students read either classical Greek or Latin after they leave college? If, with all this labor, we fail to imbue our young men with a love for the classics, is there any reason to fear that any change will render their position less advantageous?[70]

From the humanistic classical education of Vittorino da Feltre and his successors to the deep personal engagement with ancient history and literature evinced in the correspondence of Jefferson and John Adams, Classics had been more than a subject to be chosen or not, and more than simply an aspect of education. In Europe and America, it had been the education of every member of the governing classes. It had provided the language, tropes, and material of public discourse and cultural dialogue.

In the new civilization that emerged in America during the first six decades of the nineteenth century, this link between classical and liberal education was severed, and in turn the link between Classics and public life dissolved. The Rockfish Gap report and the Yale Report of 1828 epitomize a debate about education that moved Classics from the center of the political arena to the margins of higher education. Whether in the Old Colleges like Yale, Princeton, Williams, or Amherst, or in a few state universities like Virginia and Michigan, Classics became a purely educational phenomenon. Once beyond formal education, the governing classes of America no longer needed or used Latin and Greek. If Classics appeared in the architecture of their thought, it was as ornament, not framework. For Tocqueville's pioneer and President Jackson alike, it was enough to know a few decorative mottoes, to mumble something in the vernacular, or to assert with Emerson the priority of "the meal in the firkin; the milk in the pan; the ballad in the street; the news of the boat; the glance of the eye; the form and gait of the body."[71]

CLASSICS IN RETREAT:
ALTERTUMSWISSENSCHAFT COMES TO AMERICA

Both the Old College and the Jeffersonian university justified their existence by appealing to what happened to their students: the Old College evoked the strengthening of mental faculties through its traditional, classical curriculum; and the Jeffersonian university expected, as the Rockfish Gap report put it, "to develop the reasoning faculties of our youth, enlarge their minds, cultivate their morals, and instill into them the precepts of virtue and order; to enlighten them with mathematical and physical sciences which advance the arts and administer to the health, the subsistence and comforts of human life; and generally to form them to habits of reflection, and correct action, rendering them examples of virtue to others and of happiness within themselves."[72] In the half century between the Civil War and World War I, however, a Germanic ideal of research, along with the growing demand for higher education to meet the needs of what the Harvard philosopher George Santayana dubbed "crude but vital America,"[73] reshaped the American university. In 1860 graduate schools, deans and provosts, departments and their chairs, did not exist; by 1900 all these things were in place, and with them the learned journals and societies, foundations, and institutes that form the ancillary apparatus of academic life. The distinctively American combination of "an undergraduate college basically English in conception . . . wedded, by loose financial ties, to a Germanic graduate school"[74] had become the norm.

From the beginning of this development classical studies occupied a central place. Although some Americans did take medical or scientific degrees in Germany, the real attraction of Germany for Americans who hoped to become scholars was its reputation for innovative, rigorous scholarship in the humanities, and the science of antiquity, *Altertumswissenschaft*, stood at the center of the humanities.[75] From the first American experience with German scholarship until the First World War, the classical scholar appears as the primary example of German scholarly superiority.

The historian George Bancroft (1800–1891), one of the first Americans to study in Germany,[76] astutely saw both the positive and negative side of German scholarship during his years at Göttingen from 1818 to 1820. On the one hand, he wrote, learning was carried on "as a trade, though an elevating and important one," and German scholars seemed to lack the elevated sense of vocation that American scholars expected; on the other hand, the disciplined labor of German researchers produced results that astonished someone used to American and English dilettantism:

> It is wonderful to see how a learned man can look back upon antiquity, how intimately he can commune with her, how he rests upon her bosom as upon the bosom of a friend. He can hear the still feeble voice, that comes from remote ages, and which is lost in the distance to common ears. The darkest portions of history become almost transparent, when reason and acuteness are united with German perseverance. It is admirable to see with what calmness and patience every author is read, every manuscript collected, every work perused, which can be useful, be it dull or interesting, the work of genius or stupidity; to see how most trifling coins and medals, the ruins of art and even the decay of nature is made to bear upon the investigated subject.[77]

Bancroft had recognized, in nearly its earliest stages, the comprehensive *Altertumswissenschaft* of Boeckh.

Bancroft and the other pioneers brought their vision of German scholarship and German universities into the debate over the direction of American higher education that was already boiling in the new republic; one of them, George Ticknor, corresponded with Jefferson about the new University of Virginia. But this first wave of Germanic scholarship broke in vain against the intractable realities of a new nation. There were no libraries adequate to support research, few scholars, and a pervasive sense that the country did not need the kind of institutional scholarship that Bancroft and the others had admired. Emerson's vision of the American scholar entailed a distinctively American scholarship shaped by nature and native intelligence more than by Germanic diligence and system: "Thought and knowledge are natures in which apparatus and pretension avail nothing. Gowns, and pecuniary foundations, though of towns of gold, can never countervail the least sentence or syllable of wit."[78] George Ticknor spent fifteen years as Smith Professor of French and Spanish Languages and professor of belles-lettres at Harvard agitating for curricular and institutional reform along Germanic lines before resigning in defeat in 1835.

In pre-Civil War American higher education, classical studies was closely identified with the fossilized curriculum of the Old College and the promotion of mental discipline advocated by the Yale Report of 1828, and even defenders of this American classical education recognized the defects of this approach; one of them describes Yale in the 1820s as a place where uninspired tutors, "generally recent graduates who had attained high distinction in their several classes, and had not yet entered on the professional careers to which most of them were destined," took every pupil thrice daily through a recitation on points of grammar and translation without any attention to literary interpretation, historical background, or cultural context.[79] Advocates of reform like Francis Wayland acknowledged that broadening the scope of the curriculum would mean the end of the Old College and so of classical studies. In this they may well have been right.

The Civil War may have saved American classical studies from oblivion. In its aftermath, a newly invigorated, confident, and industrialized nation could look to European models of higher education and expect that it could emulate and perhaps even surpass them. While memories of the Revolution and War of 1812 were still fresh, Americans chose German universities rather than Oxford or Cambridge.[80] A new cadre of German-trained classical scholars like Basil Lanneau Gildersleeve (Ph.D. Göttingen 1853), Albert Harkness (Ph.D. Bonn 1854), and William Watson Goodwin (Ph.D. Göttingen 1854) was ready to take its place in new kinds of institutions supported by industrial capital; Gildersleeve, who has some claim to be considered the founder of modern American classical scholarship, became the first professor of Greek at the new Johns Hopkins University. This prewar generation of German-trained Ph.D.s was followed by others like Paul Shorey (Ph.D. Munich 1884) and William Abbott Oldfather (Ph.D. Munich 1908) until the First World War put a temporary end to Germanic influence on American scholarship.[81] Until the end of the nineteenth century, Americans made up the largest group of foreign students in Germany, and men (and some women, like Bryn Mawr's first president, M. Carey Thomas) with German doctorates dominated American academic life.[82]

Once under way, the transformation of American academic life was rapid. In 1886, for example, the undergraduate program at the University of Pennsylvania still followed very much the model of the Old College. During their four years, the students followed a uniform, mostly classical course of study. Knowledge of Greek was required for admission, and study of it continued through the undergraduate program. In that year the students of Pennsylvania put on a production of Aristophanes' *Acharnians*, in Greek, to great popular acclaim in both Philadelphia and New York.[83] Remarkable as it may seem, no one connected with the Philadelphia *Acharnians* was what now would be recognized as a professional classicist. No one in the cast was a Greek major because there were no Greek majors, no department of Classics, and indeed hardly any differentiation of undergraduate studies according to discipline, at the University of Pennsylvania in 1886.

In 1886 the disciplinary apparatus of classical studies and modern professional academic life was only in its infancy, if indeed it existed at all. In the quarter century following the Civil War, the idea of a research university organized along disciplinary lines emerged only gradually from debate about the appropriate place of collegiate studies in American life. Of the older universities, only Harvard under Charles W. Eliot seemed in 1886 to be moving toward the modern pattern. Yale under Noah Porter, Princeton under James McCosh, and Columbia under Frederick A. P. Barnard still adhered in varying degrees to the British traditions and amateur, humane, fundamentally classical curriculum of the Old Colleges. Daniel Coit Gilman's ideas for a research-oriented, graduate institution, The Johns Hopkins University, remained an experiment anxiously watched and debated since its foundation in 1876. Stanford and The University of Chicago were still in the future when the *Acharnians* went on in Philadelphia. Departments and graduate schools came into being only gradually during the late 1880s and 1890s, although a few autonomous departments existed at Cornell and Johns Hopkins as early as 1880. (At the University of Pennsylvania in the 1880s, "department" referred to what nowadays would be called a school, like the "Department of Law," "Department of Medicine," or "College Department." The earliest department in the modern sense seems to have been the Biological Department, founded in 1882 as an outgrowth of the Department of Medicine.) Harvard's graduate school, founded in 1875, may have been as much an attempt to preempt graduate-oriented Johns Hopkins as a reflection of enthusiasm for advanced study and research; Penn's graduate school followed in 1882.[84] The American Philological Association, the nation's oldest learned society linked to an academic discipline, was only seventeen years old in 1886, and its original concept of "philology" still covered far more than what we now think of as classical studies. By 1903, when the students of the University of Pennsylvania attempted an *Iphigeneia in Tauris*, all this had changed.

The early 1890s saw an academic boom. Enrollments expanded in existing colleges, and increasing numbers of colleges and universities oriented toward research were founded; Clark, Stanford, and the University of Chicago, all founded between 1889 and 1892, exemplify this trend. The new institutions filled with undergraduates of a different kind, the sons—and increasingly, the daughters—of families who

viewed collegiate education as a path upward in society and as preparation for success in business or professional life, not as an entitlement or
a necessary first step toward an assured social position, to which one's
profession was an adjunct. By 1900, the old classical curriculum and its
distinctive feature, compulsory Greek, had given way to the elective
system, which served this new population and, coincidentally, allowed
its teachers to focus their efforts on specialized research.[85] In the newly
specialized, departmentalized American university, with its elective curriculum and prestigious graduate school, classical studies became one
specialty among many. Its practitioners became specialists themselves,
philologists or historians or epigraphists or papyrologists. In 1880
Gildersleeve reviewed a production of Aeschylus's *Agamemnon* at
Oxford. His review suggested that such productions might heal the
growing rift between "the hold that the great poets of antiquity have on
the popular mind" and classical philology, the "deeper knowledge . . .
vouchsafed only to those who make it a special study."[86] The gap that
Gildersleeve saw only grew wider, as those with the deeper knowledge
talked more and more among themselves, and less and less to the "popular mind."

Yet even as it moved further away from public life, American classical scholarship rapidly attained parity with its German model. By
1900, American graduate schools were training Ph.D.s whose accomplishments equaled those of their colleagues in Germany, and many
American scholars had earned European reputations. Between 1885,
when Gildersleeve published his edition of Pindar's *Olympians*, and
1914, when John Williams White's edition of the scholia to
Aristophanes' *Birds* appeared, German *Altertumswissenschaft* transformed classical studies in America.[87]

The effects of this transformation were both good and bad. Classical
studies moved away from the dilettantism and gerund grinding that had
characterized American colleges before the Civil War. It is unfortunate,
however, that the period of Germany's greatest influence on American
classical studies coincided with the scholarly generation between
Boeckh (1785–1867) and Wilamowitz (1848–1931), and that the

dominant strand of German influence in that era can be traced to Göttingen, an institution that emphasized specialized study of minor details and neglected the comprehensive tradition of Boeckh. From the 1880s until World War I, American classical scholars concentrated their efforts on concordances, editions of minor works, and narrowly focused grammatical study. In a country where libraries big enough to support extensive research were still few and far between, such projects flourished. Gildersleeve, who had heard Boeckh's final lectures, is the exception that proves this generalization. He argued passionately throughout his life for a comprehensive classical scholarship that would engage the cultural life of America, yet he had to admit that American scholars were "too much given to arid speculation."[88]

LOSING GROUND

Thus when Jaeger came to America, he found a form of classical studies very different from the comprehensive *Altertumswissenschaft* that he had known and practiced in Germany. American classical studies had succeeded in developing a tradition of competent, useful scholarship — editions, concordances, catalogs, and meticulous studies of detailed points of interpretation.[89] Archaeology, epigraphy, and papyrology, supported by the wealth of American universities and foundations and buoyed by the glamour of artifacts and expeditions, became particular strengths of American classical scholarship.[90] Yet there were things that Americans did not do. Works of broad cultural synthesis like Jaeger's *Paedeia*, comprehensive interpretation like Ronald Syme's *Tacitus*, or global analysis like Michael Rostovtzeff's history of Rome tended to come from elsewhere: either from refugees and exiles like Jaeger and Rostovtzeff, or from British scholars like Syme. If one looks for Americans who produced scholarship of comparable breadth and quality, one finds either naturalized citizens like Gilbert Highet or expatriates like Moses Finley. Classical scholars educated and working in America did not, for the most part, handle big ideas, ask large questions, or engage in dialogue with their own society and culture.

This self-imposed triviality rose out of the very nature of the American polity to which European classical education was imported. It is not simply a matter of America never having known the hand of Rome. Our founding fathers, despite their deep acquaintance with Greece and Rome and the influence of those cultures upon them, succeeded in establishing an unclassical nation. Our fundamental ideology, created by the Declaration's assertion that highly debatable truths are self-evident, denies the premises of classical humanism and the education created to transmit it.

In this revolutionary new nation, every traditional art and every academic discipline had to justify itself and find its distinctive American form. Literature, in the generation of Whitman and Melville, succeeded in doing so; classical studies never did. The debate over the place of classical studies in the new Republic might have led to the creation of a distinctively American classical education if the advocates of classical education had not chosen to define it in terms of the educational theory of the Old College and to link the study of Latin and Greek with the idea of developing mental faculties. In this linking, the Yale Report of 1828 was both representative and influential. As higher education struggled to develop its distinctive American form, advocates of reform like Francis Wayland could assume with reason that creating an American education would mean the end of classical studies.

In one way, the coming of *Altertumswissenschaft* saved classical studies in America. But by successfully embracing this import, classical studies cut itself off from another important debate. The very success of scholarship on the German pattern, not only in Classics but in other fields as well, produced an inevitable reaction. In the last decade of the nineteenth century and the first third of the twentieth, critics of what seemed the sterile positivism and excessive specialization of research, especially in the humanities, began to call for a new kind of undergraduate education aimed at inculcating liberal culture and developing what they called "the whole man." In the early days of this debate, its advocates sometimes made a link between liberal culture and classical, especially Greek, civilization,[91] but as the debate went on, that link became ever more tenuous. Classicists did little to strengthen it. Amateur classicists of the old school opposed the new liberal education because, with its multiple courses of study based on a generalized psychology, it rejected the rigid classical education of the Old College. Progressive, professional classicists opposed it because it was incompatible with their rigorous study of the ancient world. "The advocates of culture," as Laurence Veysey says, "had to gain their ground not only against the old-time classicists but also against the philologists, who at this very time were seeking to convert the study of language into a science."[92] Thus Classics excluded itself from American liberal arts education and from any but a marginal place in its characteristic institution, the liberal arts college. English, a newer field unburdened by the past or by the necessity of learning at least two difficult languages, could succeed where Classics failed and become the default humanity.

Among themselves, classicists developed two false paradigms of American education. Both depended on a distorted vision of European precedent. On the one hand, *Altertumswissenschaft* in the mode of Göttingen emphasized verbal trees at the expense of cultural forests; on the other, an Anglophile, aesthetic idea of liberal education, fed by the myth of an Oxbridge Golden Age when everyone studied Classics and sixth form boys read Juvenal at sight, made a fetish of language and literature and pushed philosophical and cultural studies to the margins of Classics. Some American scholars regarded A. E. Housman as an ideal classical scholar, and it became possible to major in Classics at an American university without ever taking a course in anything but poetry.[93]

Classical education in America began as a mirror of the Old World, became a ground of debate, then a measure of anxiety, and ended as an academic irrelevancy, unsure of its place in American education and susceptible to ideological attacks from all sides. Because classical studies had never become naturalized in America, it would become vulnerable to the reflection of European debates over the theoretical grounds of humane study; because American classicists were not after all engaged in the same practice as their European counterparts, they have been able to blunt, but never to refute, criticism of their lack of relevance to American education. Even at the beginning of the twenty-first century, it is possible to imagine the demise of classical studies in America.

Chapter 3

FINIS:
FOUR ARGUMENTS AGAINST CLASSICS

Dying, the old woman traveled back to the beginning of her life. It had been just after the beginning of the century that was now drawing to a close. Ninety years, more, ago. In her journey she heard her mother recalling the millennial hysteria, the, what did she call it, California silliness, that had swept through newspapers and magazines. Newspapers. How odd to think of those, now. She remembered her grandfather. A Latin teacher. A classical scholar, as they still said then. Odder even than a newspaper, to think of a Latin teacher. Her great-grandchildren, bright little persons, she'd asked them about Latin, none of them had ever heard of it, not in their schools or anyone else's, maybe a few people somewhere knew it. The books were still upstairs, in their boxes.

C. S. Lewis is supposed to have remarked that if you wanted to find a man who could not read Vergil in Latin, although his father could, you would have a much better chance of success in the twentieth century A.D. than in the ninth. I think it entirely possible that if my great-great-great-grandchildren want to learn a classical language really well, there will be no college or university in which they can do so. Perhaps they will teach themselves or find someone who can teach them informally, in the way that it is now possible to learn calligraphy, or heraldry, or how to use an astrolabe. Or they may be able to find in

85

a few universities specialists in this forgotten language, which will occupy a place next to Akkadian or ancient Sumerian. If Latin disappears from formal higher education, as ancient Greek nearly has already,[1] it will be because four arguments, each reinforcing the others, have prevailed.

FIRST ARGUMENT: UTILITY AND VALUE

The first argument holds that because the study of Latin no longer serves any social function, Latin should no longer be studied. In one sense this is not an argument so much as a statement of fact. When Latin or any subject ceases to have a function in society, it will no longer find a place in the education sponsored by that society. The statement only becomes an argument when, as now, the function of a subject is at issue because the social and intellectual changes that may lead to its disappearance are not yet complete.

The argument takes two forms. The first is naïve and easily countered. It holds that because a person who knows Latin knows no skill or knowledge that has a use as such, no person need study Latin. What is Latin good for? What is its practical value? These and similar questions assume that the utility of knowledge is the same as its value and, further, that useful knowledge can only be knowledge that leads directly to action in or on the world. But many kinds of knowledge have a value without having a use. Trigonometry or calculus have no use in the lives of most people, but hardly anyone denies their value: as structures of beauty, as essential parts of other kinds of knowledge that do have value or utility, or as exercises that make it easier to acquire other kinds of valuable or useful knowledge. If one must have utility as a criterion, it is easy enough to justify trigonometry or Latin as courses that improve one's chances of attaining higher socioeconomic status by gaining a prestigious degree, a high SAT score, or some other mark of educational distinction.

The naïve observation that knowing Latin has no utility, also, proceeds from the erroneous assumption that the sole point of education is to know things. Sometimes it is, but more often the point of education is to learn things. The value of many subjects, that is, lies in what they do to students' minds, not in their content. Knowing Latin is useful to only a few people; learning Latin may be useful to many more.

The second form of this first argument is more subtle. It is not about knowledge, but about the social production of it, about education. All education, the first argument suggests, serves some function in society; Newman's notion of university education as the pursuit of "knowledge for its own sake" conceals the real nature of universities as social institutions engaged in transmitting and producing knowledge and through that production preserving the structures and ideologies of dominant authority. "Culture," one Marxist observed, "serves authority, and ultimately the national State, not because it represses and coerces but because it is affirmative, positive, and persuasive."[2] Just as Newman ignored his contemporary Marx, so those who have inherited his role as advocate of the liberal arts ignore the various Marxist understandings of knowledge production as part of the cultural superstructure built on the economic base of society.[3] If knowledge is a commodity, its factories and markets will look like universities.

Although Marxist thinkers have produced the most sophisticated theoretical understanding of education in terms of the social and economic relations that make up society, non-Marxists also like the concept. "The marketplace of ideas" is a cliché in the publicity of American universities, as is emphasis on the relation between higher education and economic value. Because the capitalist marketplace appears to be self-regulating, it occurs as a natural metaphor in the thought of the presidents, deans, and other academic bureaucrats who hope for a university that will also be self-regulating—managed, not governed.

Latin, then, and by extension the study of Classics as a whole, both true liberal arts and true *Altertumswissenschaft*, can be seen as a cultural superstructure that has become alienated from its socieconomic base. The self-conscious governing class whose tastes, values, and attitudes classical education was intended to form has vanished, and with it the social function of that education.

Some of the justifications once offered for classical education now confront a reader with their strangeness. Casual documents from minor players often reveal more than formal, analytical justifications like Newman's. William DeWitt Hyde, president of Bowdoin College from 1885 to 1917, once set down in rhythmic prose what he called "The Promise of the College."

> To be at home in all lands and all ages;
> To count Nature a familiar acquaintance,
> And Art an intimate friend;
> To gain a standard for the appreciation of other men's work
> And the criticism of one's own:
> To carry the keys of the world's library in one's pocket
> And feel its resources behind one in whatever task he
>   undertakes;
> To make hosts of friends among the men of one's own age
> Who are to be leaders in all walks of life;
> To lose oneself in generous enthusiasms
> And co-operate with others for common ends;
> To learn manners from students who are gentlemen,
> And form character under professors who are Christians —
> This is the offer of the college for the best four years of one's
>   life.[4]

Even though it was published only a century ago, this is a document from a vanished world, not only because it uses so naturally the cadences of the King James Bible and the Book of Common Prayer, but also because it takes for granted so much that hardly anyone now accepts. The assumptions that students are uniformly men and gentlemen and that professors are Christians leap off the page, but other guiding principles seem equally astounding upon examination: that capitalized Art and Nature can be domesticated as "familiar acquaintance" or "intimate friend," or that a unitary standard of appreciation and criticism exists and can be acquired. But as surely as any Marxist, and more surely than many of his successors in the bureaucratic university of the late twentieth century, President Hyde recognized the socio-economic base of classical, liberal education. One of its purposes was to bring together prospective members of the governing class—"men of one's own age who are to be leaders in all walks of life"—and to create networks of friendship among them.

When liberal education lost this purpose, classical education lost its reason for existence. The kind of literacy it inculcated ceased to matter. Again, a document intended to inspire those already committed to participate in classical education will reveal much about the assumptions implicit in that social practice. William Johnson Cory, a nineteenth-century master in Classics at Eton,[5] explained the aims of Etonian education in this way:

> You go to school at the age of twelve or thirteen; and for the next four or five years you are not engaged so much in acquiring knowledge as in making mental efforts under criticism. A certain amount of knowledge you can indeed with average faculties acquire so as to retain; nor need you regret the hours that you spent on much that is forgotten, for the shadow of lost knowledge at least protects you from many illusions. But you go to a great school not for knowledge so much as for arts and habits;
>
> for the habit of attention,
> for the art of expression,
> for the art of assuming at a moment's notice a new intellectual posture,
> for the art of entering quickly into another person's thoughts,
> for the habit of submitting to censure or refutation,
> for the art of indicating assent or dissent in graduated terms,
> for the habit of regarding minute points of accuracy,
> for the habit of working out what is possible in a given time,
> for taste,
> for discrimination,
> for mental courage and mental soberness.
> Above all, you go to a great school for self-knowledge.

Note the assumptions built into Cory's exhortation. Education does not aim at knowledge, understood as the acquisition of facts. Instead, arts and habits, what a later age might call internalized knowledge, constitute the goal of an Eton education. The structure of Cory's list, carefully arranged in a longer group of eight items followed by a shorter group of four, calls attention to this internalization by modeling it. Each of the first eight items is marked as either art or habit, then named with an easily understood noun ("attention, expression") or given a clear definition ("entering quickly into another person's thoughts, submitting to censure or refutation"). The last four items, in contrast, offer no purchase to anyone not already inside the system in which they have meaning. The first three form an ascending tricolon, each clause longer than the one preceding. Taste and discrimination can be recognized only by those who already have them. Mental courage and mental soberness differ, as the emphatic repetition of the adjective suggests, from ordinary courage and soberness; like taste and discrimination, they cannot be apprehended or appreciated by those who do not already know the code in which they are expressed. All higher primates know what fear is,[6] and any person who recognizes fear can recognize its reciprocal, physical courage; recognizing mental courage, on the other hand, depends on having some sense of what one might or might not be afraid to think—of the taboos and customs of a particular class or society.

Finally, Cory ends his list with "self-knowledge," the ultimate goal of education for a governing class learning to be, above all things, aware of itself and intentional in performing its function in society. Self-knowledge, by definition, can only be apprehended by the self that is both its subject and object, its doer and its thing done. In the same way, Cory's list embodies the tropes of the classical rhetoric taught in the education that it advocates; the list is what it is about. At its climax stands the enclosed, self-reflexive, completely internalized knowledge and rhetoric of the classically educated governing class, whose ways remain closed to those who have not passed through its schools.

Cory's twelve points imply a specific kind of literary and linguistic curriculum. Accuracy and attention to detail, censure and refutation, assent or dissent carefully expressed in graduated terms, entering into another person's character, and the working out of an exercise in a given time all formed part of a pupil's work in Renaissance grammar schools, and in all schools derived from them. In Latin compositions and orations students praised noble Lucretia or blamed adulterous Helen, assumed the character of Alexander before the tomb of Achilles, and argued the merits of sententious propositions from Cato or Plautus, while the masters assessed their command of Latin grammar and classical rhetoric. As surely as Newman in the passage from his seventh *Discourse on the Idea of a University* quoted above, Cory speaks for and from a specific kind of literacy dedicated to the service of a specific social class. When that class disappeared, the need for its literacy disappeared with it. To many people, whether from nostalgia or from taste, that literacy and its products remain attractive. They cannot, to anyone who accepts the first argument against the study of Latin, continue to be important.

SECOND ARGUMENT: ELITES AND ELITISM

The second argument against the study of Latin focuses on what actually happens in classrooms when students encounter a subject whose social and economic foundations have eroded. Latin, this argument maintains, has ceased to be a subject for an elite and has become a subject merely elitist. The sheer difficulty of learning classical languages, along with the traditions of pedagogy by which they are usually taught, impose a barrier that excludes all but a few students who have the leisure and mental qualities necessary to learn them. The demand that serious students of Greece and Rome develop high competency in Greek and Latin, Martin Bernal has remarked, "is a very effective barrier to keep out strangers, who have not been properly taught the ways in which the members of the discipline think."[7]

The persuasiveness of this second argument depends on what is meant by difficulty and on a much harder question: who exactly is excluded and who admitted by the difficulties inherent in learning a classical language? Difficulty as applied to mental operations is both subjective and cultural. The difficulty of mental operations is subjectively determined. When we say that some mental operation is difficult, we mean that most people cannot perform it without becoming aware that they are doing so.[8] The more uncomfortable that self-awareness becomes, the greater the difficulty of the mental operation that produced it. The difficulty of mental operations is also culturally ordered. What constitutes a difficult operation for a person depends on the person's culture, social status, trade, degree and manner of education, and so on. In middle-class American society, most people find it difficult to do calculations involving fractions smaller than one-eighth or bases other than ten. Carpenters calculate in sixteenths or even thirty-seconds, and practiced celestial navigators find it easy to calculate in sexagesimal degrees, minutes, and seconds.

Learning Latin by the traditional approach, which is rooted in the pedagogical practices of Renaissance grammar schools, might almost have been designed to make one uncomfortably aware that one is learning Latin. Consider the process encoded in F. M. Wheelock's *Introduction to Latin*, perhaps the most widely used elementary text in American colleges and universities and in countless, or at least uncounted, other textbooks. First, a student learns a paradigm, a pattern for the changes that one class of words undergoes in various contexts. Then the student learns a number of words, the vocabulary of the chapter. For each word the student must learn not only the word's meaning, but also information necessary to inflect or change the word into its various forms; for nouns, for example, the student must learn each noun's nominative singular, genitive singular, gender, and meaning. Then the student reads, marks, learns, and inwardly digests an explanation of syntax, adding this new information to a structure of grammar that has been gradually built up over the course of the previous lessons. Finally, the student applies paradigms, vocabulary, and grammar in sentences. Some sentences are in Latin, and they must be translated into English; some are in English, to be translated into Latin.

Even the simplest such translation requires intensive, conscious analysis and almost obsessive attention to logic and detail. "The song was short," a student sees in the English-to-Latin section of his book. Song. That's the subject of the sentence, therefore nominative case in Latin. The sentence speaks of one song, therefore nominative singular of the word for song. *Carmen.* Is. The subject of the sentence is neither I nor you, and so the verb is third person, not first or second. Singular, and "is" in English comes from the verb "to be," which in Latin is *sum*, *esse*, *fui*, an irregular verb. *est.* "Short." Predicate adjective, therefore nominative, agreeing with *carmen*, therefore singular, and *carmen*, *carminis* belongs to the category or gender of nouns called neuter, therefore neuter. *breve. Carmen est breve.* Got it. I hope.

This grammar-translation method, as it is called, is a very inefficient way to learn a foreign language, and it is no surprise that most people, especially adults, who study Latin in this way develop no fluency in the language. Teachers of French or German are often astonished to learn that after two years of Latin in college, students can read only limited amounts of an ancient author, perhaps twenty or thirty pages, in a semester, that they can write the language only with very great difficulty, and that they can speak it not at all.[9] Latin teachers have grown accustomed to explaining why their students seem to know so little; William Cory, in the passage quoted above, justifies "the hours spent on much that is forgotten" by appealing to the prophylactic value of "the shadow of lost knowledge."

Why not, then, teach and learn Latin in a different, more efficient way by adapting for Latin the very successful techniques used to teach French or Spanish? To some extent this has been done. Both the oral-aural and the reading-in-context methods of teaching Latin have long had their advocates.[10] Latin students in the Renaissance learned to speak Latin as they studied its grammar. Over seventy years ago a report of the American Classical League gushed, "the indispensable primary immediate objective in the study of Latin is progressive development of ability to read and understand Latin."[11] Pronunciation, knowledge of vocabulary, syntax, and forms, and the ability to translate Latin into English and English into Latin appeared as secondary objectives. Early editions of one very successful textbook of the 1970s (the

Cambridge Latin Course) dispensed with grammatical terms like "case," although the objections of teachers and the demands of the market brought the traditional terminology back to later editions. Composition, the practice of translating English into Latin, which formed an indispensable part of traditional classical education in Britain and America, has come especially under attack in recent years. Its critics raise the charge of "elitism," and the predictable point that there is no practical reason to be able to write anything in Latin.[12] Composition is difficult and pointless, they say; it should be discarded.

Both these critics and the pedagogical theorists who maintain that reading Latin literature is the goal of studying Latin share with advocates of the traditional method of teaching Latin a conviction that everyone ought to have access to the study of Latin. An evenhanded survey of the state of Latin teaching in American schools and colleges concludes with a series of recommendations, of which this is the first:

> In an age when the need to communicate effectively is critical, all students can benefit from the study of Latin. We must take them all with whatever deficiencies they may have, and try to structure programs that offer the best opportunity for some degree of success to every student. This includes many groups that have not traditionally studied Latin: "Limited English Proficiency" students, Learning Disabled students, the economically and culturally disadvantaged, the handicapped, and students "at-risk."[13]

It would now be difficult to find a Latin teacher, no matter what his or her pedagogical convictions, who did not endorse this admirable inclusivity.

The second argument, then, seems to be in danger of collapsing. Widespread adoption of teaching methods not grounded in the educational culture of a Renaissance elite has mitigated the particular difficulty of learning Latin. Even those who, for whatever reasons, continue to teach in the traditional style reject the elitism that went with it, and they have in many cases discarded the most rebarbative features of that style.

These changes, the second argument responds, do not matter. They do not touch the deep, intractable elitism of Latin itself, no matter what the method by which it is taught or the intentions of the teacher. Whether considered as historical phenomenon or as system of representation, Latin embodies all that we mean by elitism: hierarchy, privilege, and exclusion. There is no way to teach it, the second argument holds, without taking into oneself the contamination of these ideas.

When I speak of "Latin" in the preceding paragraph, I do not mean any and all actual and possible utterances in the Latin language. I refer instead to the curricular subject called "Latin" in twentieth-century schools and colleges, and to the subset of these utterances from which it is derived: the surviving writings of Cicero, Caesar, Vergil, Ovid, Livy, and other authors of the first centuries B.C. and A.D. These classical texts, which are essential to the subject called Latin, cannot be separated from the elitism that engendered them.[14] Nor can the language in which they are written, and its grammar.

If it were simply a matter of distancing oneself from the values expressed or implicit in these texts and their conditions of authorship, from their endorsement or tacit acceptance of slavery, oligarchy, or militarism, then it would not be difficult to read these works against their grain, so to speak, and to teach them without complicity in their values. But their elitism goes deeper than that. The difficulty of Latin turns out to be built into the language itself. The elitist barriers cannot be torn down without destroying the very thing to which they seemed to block access. Even when pedagogy in the Latin classroom becomes open, democratic, and accessible, Latin itself remains closed, hierarchical, and difficult.

It remains so because Latin, as I have defined it above, represents only part of the language of the Romans. Latin the curricular subject preserves the public language of the Roman governing class. This class consciously developed a language that not only expressed its will to power, but also was itself an instrument for carrying out that will. Learning Latin means internalizing a language whose historical users shaped it as an instrument of civic domination.

Nowhere is this clearer than in Cicero's *Brutus*, a dramatic dialogue written in 46 B.C. near the end of Cicero's life, when the oligarchic ruling class of the Roman Republic was on the point of destroying itself in civil war. Cicero was not by birth a member of the inner circle of this Roman governing class. Assiduous study, constant practice, a genius for rhetoric, and keen political instincts had brought him to the consulship and to a place among the leaders of the senate. The collapse of the system under which he had risen to prominence, and with it his hopes and ambitions, prompted Cicero to reflect on the history of rhetoric, the tool with which, he knew, he had reached his position in the state.[15]

Like many outsiders, Cicero was able to look at the structures of power with a clarity often denied to the native. In *Brutus* he puts forward a sustained argument for the power of rhetoric to sustain a benevolent oligarchy. His words gain effectiveness from his melancholy acceptance of the fact that the coming anarchy will make all his arguments, and indeed all persuasion, useless.

Cicero sees oratory as a weapon in politics during stable times: "For me too it is a source of deep pain that the state feels no need of those weapons of counsel, of insight, and of authority, which I had learned to handle and to rely upon, —weapons which are the peculiar and proper resource of a leader in the commonwealth and of a civilized and law-abiding state" (*Brutus* 7).[16] He uses Periclean Athens as his example of the correlation between advances in eloquence and civil harmony (*Brutus* 45), but he does not associate the public eloquence of the Roman governing class with democratic polities like that of fifth-century Athens. His conjectural account of oratory in the early Republic (*Brutus* 52–57) emphasizes the role of rhetoric in securing the privileges of an oligarchic governing class against tyrannical kings on the one hand and turbulent people on the other. When he has to treat antioligarchic orators like Tiberius Gracchus and Gaius Carbo, he denies them the highest level of *gloria*, the Roman oligarchy's word for the rewards for which it competed (*Brutus* 103).

In Cicero's vision of the Roman commonwealth of discourse, rhetoric creates a relationship between speaker and audience that reflects and creates the Roman governing class's ideal relationship between governors and governed. Cicero argues that the quality of an orator can only be judged by what his oratory effects; that is, by changes in his audience's behavior (*Brutus* 183ff.). The audience, however, exercises judgments that are created by the orator's manipulation of them. Hence popular judgments of an orator inevitably coincide with expert opinion. In this model of critical judgment, the popular audience is a passive tool in the hands of the oratorical governor, like a wind instrument or a trained horse (*Brutus* 192). The limited participation of the mass of citizens in Roman politics finds a reflection in Cicero's model of audience response.

Cicero constructs a narrative in which the development of rhetoric in Latin goes hand in hand with the development of the Roman Republic's oligarchic institutions. Along with this instrumental, oligarchic discourse grew the concept of "Latinity," *Latinitas*. Standards of correctness in grammar and usage became part of the Roman governing class's construction of itself. During the first century B.C. that class hunted out and purged from the language of public life every locution that smacked of the peasant or the foreigner.[17] The need to purify Latin itself from these degenerate influences could be justified in the terms of the Roman oligarchy's master narrative, which told of a pure and primitive commonwealth, in which every man knew his place, corrupted by an influx of foreign wealth and manners. As Cicero puts it:

> But at that time nearly everyone who lived outside the capital and had not been stained by some native barbarism spoke Latin correctly. But the passage of time made that situation worse, both at Rome and in Greece, for into both Athens and this city flowed many people from a variety of places who spoke a defiled Latin; all the more reason to purify our speech (*Brutus* 258).

This purification proceeded on two fronts: careful pronunciation on the one hand, and on the other, choice of vocabulary and attention to grammatical structures like case, number, gender, and tense.[18] As they developed a formal grammar to cleanse and regularize their language, the Roman governing class of the first century B.C. followed systems that

Alexandrian grammarians had promulgated under the influence of Stoic ideas about language and meaning.[19] In this area as in so many others, Roman classicism looking to Greek models became the West's classical standard. This purified Latin and its grammar, both idiolect and instrument of government, is what students learn when they learn Latin.

This curricular subject called Latin preserves and signifies the way in which the Roman governing class constructed its society and its world. It dominates, orders, controls, and arranges into a hierarchy all that it touches. Even the elementary step in grammar of ordering words into paradigms presents the learner with a world in which the acting subject, the nominative, precedes the object of action, the accusative, and the first person, I, is prior to the second, you, and to the third that is all others. "The world of language," as Teresa Morgan describes it, "revolves around the singular subject, whose relations with others are then determined primarily by distance, greater proximity leading to greater intimacy."[20] Grammatical as well as actual roads all lead to Rome, the ruler of the distant and the unlettered.

Again, Cicero bears witness to this epistemological imperialism. Speaking of his friend Sulpicius Rufus, who brought order to the study of civil law, he writes:

> This [making civil law an art] he could never have attained through knowledge of the law alone had he not acquired in addition that art which teaches the analysis of a whole into its component parts, sets forth and defines the latent and implicit, interprets and makes clear the obscure; which first recognizes the ambiguous and then distinguishes; which applies in short a rule or measure for adjudging truth and falsehood, for determining what conclusions follow from what premises, and what do not. This art, the mistress of all arts, he brought to bear on all that had been put together by others without system, whether in the form of legal opinions or in actual trials (*Brutus* 152–53).

Analysis, clarity, a sharp sense of the difference between truth and falsehood, and logical reasoning have been admired, as Cicero admires them here. For him, and for many still, they represent the difference between light and darkness; a more literal translation of the last sentence might run, "This art, of all arts the greatest, he cast as, so to speak, a light on all. . . ."

For advocates of the second argument against Latin, however, this light shines cruelly on a world marked by the divisive insistence that to praise and accept the truth means to condemn and exclude what is false, by the oppressive valuation of totality and generalization over difference and particularity, and by systems of power that depend on the social realization of epistemological privilege. Feminist critics, both from inside the profession of classical studies and from without, have offered the most eloquent statements of this argument. During the 1970s the French feminists Luce Irigaray, Hélène Cixous, and Julia Kristeva developed an account of the relation between language and patriarchy that emphasizes the role of language in creating and maintaining what more conventional feminists have seen as purely social or political oppressions.[21] For Irigaray, Cixous, Kristeva, and those influenced by them, language itself creates those oppressions, and they cannot be separated from it.

Latin, the strong form of our second argument holds, presents an especially clear and enduring case of the unbreakable link between language and the oppressions of elitist patriarchy. The very qualities that Cicero admired—analysis, clarity, a sharp sense of the irreducible difference between truth and falsehood, and logical reasoning—constitute the cognitive workings of logocentric patriarchy. Cicero and his fellow patriarchs of the Roman governing class successfully forged a new, potent idiolect within the language of the Romans. In this new form they encoded their power, and with its rhetoric as their instrument they maintained control of their society and excluded from its governance all that was different, unreasonable, obscure, or alien. Their nearly total success can be measured by the persistence of their language in societies whose governance is similarly constituted. Latin has maintained its power in the educational curricula of the governing classes of Western society, the second argument insists, because the fit is so good between *Latinitas* and patriarchy.[22]

THIRD ARGUMENT: LIES ABOUT THE WORLD

The first argument, based on Latin's lack of utility, and the second, based on the social, political, and psychological implications of its difficulty, are almost commonplace. Critics of classical studies both within and outside the community of professional classicists have articulated them with varying emphases and varying degrees of enthusiasm. The third argument has seldom found explicit articulation. It is implicit in the hostility often expressed by advocates of the second argument in its strong form toward philology, the ancient, grammatical core of both liberal arts education and *Altertumswissenschaft*. Rather than talk of philology in general, I will again use Latin—not the actual language of the Romans, but the curricular subject called Latin—as the exemplary target of argument.

The third argument holds that Latin does positive harm to the intellectual development of young people. Studying Latin, this argument holds (or would hold, if any of Latin's critics were bold enough to articulate it in this strong form), means internalizing and learning the reality of certain concepts: case, number, gender, person, tense, mood, voice. At one level, these concepts seem merely grammatical—schoolteachers' harmless fictions set up to organize a difficult subject for their students.

Yet grammar, as the Stoics knew, cannot be divorced from metaphysics. All our descriptions of the world, whether physical, ethical, or logical, depend on propositions set forth in language.[23] Hence the wise person must be a dialectician, concerned with topics of signification and utterance, including predication, cases, correct usage, and other grammatical topics.[24] What kind of wisdom do the fictions of grammar teach?

They teach, our third argument holds, an image of the world that cannot any longer be believed. The traditional categories of grammar describe a world in which things are distinct from actions and subjects cannot be confused with objects. A subject, students learn, is what a sentence is about. A predicate is what is said about the subject. The two parts, subject and predicate, interact in an essential act of thought: predication, asserting something about our world.

Yet it seems clear that, however good this model may be at describing how sentences work, it cannot account for everything about the relationship between language and the world. Language appears as a series of entities—phonemes, morphemes, words, phrases, clauses, sentences—which can be recognized as distinct. In some way these distinct entities can be arranged so as to convey meaning. Their articulation seems to be governed by definite laws and hierarchies.

The world apart from language, however, resists these laws and hierarchies; it proves especially resistant to the distinction between subject and predicate. The phenomenal world does not consist of things on the one hand and on the other that which is said about them, their properties. A sentence like "The table is round" does not accurately represent the state of things regarding that table. In the world as it presents itself to our senses the table's roundness has no separate existence. Nor does the table exist apart from its roundness and its other properties. Language forces us to treat "is round" as something apart from "the table," something said about it.

Our human condition is made tragic by the fact that we must exist as grammatical beings in an ungrammatical world. A human who could construct no propositions about the world would be no human being at all, yet our innate power to construct propositions puts a veil of meanings between us and the world. We can only say things about the world. We will never be able to say the world itself.

From the Greeks onward, philosophy in the West has wrestled with this relationship between things and their qualities, and between the world and what we say about it. Plato and Aristotle, each in a different way, argued that qualities were as real as things, so that the act of predication could be an accurate representation of the world of being. The Stoics, who in their ideas about language now seem in many ways the most perceptive of the ancient schools, took a more complicated view of predication, maintaining that it created an indissoluble unit of meaning, the *lekton* or "sayable," through which it is possible to gain an accurate representation of reality.

With the possible exception of the Stoics, all philosophies of the ancient world located meaning in the structure of the world. In all these systems concepts of grammar represent this structure, and the relationships implied by case, number, gender, tense, and the rest do in fact hold in the world outside language. There are nouns and verbs because there are in fact things and actions; adjectives exist because things have qualities; past and future are as real, as much out there, as the present.

Early modern European philosophy, in contrast, located meaning in the structures of the human mind. Descartes, Kant, and those who argued with them all saw meaning as a kind of template imposed on reality by ideas or concepts. These mental entities mediate between the world and our perception of it; they, and not the world itself, are what we talk about when we use language. Mental activity becomes the warrant for existence, and the Cartesian *ego* certifies meaning: *cogito, ergo sum.*

When meaning becomes a matter of ideas in the mind, grammar changes its nature. Instead of describing an external reality in which things, actions, qualities, time, and other linguistic concepts have their being, grammar now maps an internal, mental reality of *a priori* ideas. Noun, Verb, Adjective, Tense, and the rest refer to ideas, to Language rather than to Greek, Latin, or any specific tongue. It becomes possible to dream of a universal grammar which might describe not the workings of one particular language, but the universal grammatical ideas contained in every human mind.[25]

Whether grammar—our account of language—corresponds to the actual state of things in the world or to the actual state of things in our minds hardly matters when we come to justify the importance of grammar in education. On either understanding, grammar will be true. When a student learns the distinction between noun and verb, or between subject and predicate, that student is learning something truthful about the way things are. A strong connection will bind grammatical study to the fundamental metaphysical description of that student's existence. Language, on these models, enables us to master the world by expressing its truth.

The third argument against the study of Latin points out, sometimes calmly and sometimes gleefully, that imperial language wears no clothes. There are no truthful propositions about the way things are, no facts of the matter to be expressed by predication, no connections between grammar and metaphysics. Grammar and metaphysics, in fact, are equally suspect. Both represent doomed, totalizing attempts to master and understand a world whose diversity forever resists all mastery and all understanding. If grammar is to be taught at all, it must be taught as one among many fictions; above all, the student must be taught to avoid at all costs internalizing the particular fictions of grammar: the distinction between thing and action, for example, or between subject and object.

These fictions are not harmless, the third argument maintains. As we learn and use them, they take on a kind of reality and shape both our selves and the structures of power with which we relate to one another. According to the French psychologist Jacques Lacan, language not only expresses, but also more fundamentally creates human personality. An infant pulls a toy toward him and says, "Here." He pushes the toy away and says, "There." These first crude acts of predication, which for Freud in *Beyond the Pleasure Principle* represented the infant's expression of already existing internal psychological states of loss and anxiety,[26] represent for Lacan the actual creation of such states and of the personality in which they function.

In Lacan's view, language creates the soul by forcing a distinction between subject and predicate. Infantile acts of predication, like the game of "Here . . . There" described by Freud, divide *ego*, the knowing subject, from the world of objects. In first experiencing itself, then, the knowing subject also experiences loss and separation. Its attempts to recover the lost unity of the world lead it to impose unity on the world through language.

Language imposes unity through the act of predication, because every predicate must contain at least one word denoting an idea which can be predicated of any subject whatever.[27] These universal ideas or "universals" have been one of philosophy's thorny problems, largely because it has seemed difficult to say how we can know something that has no existence as a specific object accessible to our senses. How, for example, can we have knowledge of "being" or "red"?

A Lacanian might respond that the problem of universals is a problem beyond human solving because it is rooted in the essential tragedy of the self created by language. The same language that creates us as beings aware of the world and ourselves makes us divided selves, creatures in a perpetual state of longing for the unattainable oneness of perfect predication. Adam, in one of our most profound myths, lived in a paradise without tense or noun; he was expelled only when he acquired knowledge. In Eden before knowledge existed, Adam declared what each animal was. He could speak the world; since the Fall, we have only been able to speak about it.

Insofar as notions like subject, predicate, noun, verb, and the other fictions of traditional grammar promote the belief that a unitary subject can make truthful assertions using universals, they induce a false psychology and a false epistemology. Yet precisely these fictions underlie not only traditional instruction in Latin and Greek, but also, the third argument points out, the descriptions of the world conveyed by the texts presented for study in those languages. Those who study Classics are led to believe in the reality of Socrates or Aeneas and in the truth or falsehood of statements about them. These beliefs are as harmful to us as the belief in the objective reality of our predications.

Lacan's psychology is of course only one example of a general assault on the Western tradition that the goal of philosophy is to offer a complete, true account of the nature of things. This assault on certainty had its origin in Hegel's phenomenology, and its recent manifestations range from Michel Foucault's exposure of the subjective, language-centered nature of the structures of power[28] to Daniel Dennett's demolition of the Cartesian theater of the mind.[29] The third argument against the study of Latin can find widespread support in cognitive science, psychology, social criticism, and the anti-metaphysical stance of postmodern philosophy.

The first three arguments, also, support each other. The argument from Latin's lack of utility points to the fact that classical education and the production of classical knowledge no longer serves any useful function in society. That function was to train a governing elite, but elitism based on a claim to special, accurate knowledge, the second argument holds, harms society, and there is no way to purge classical studies of it. Its roots are deep in the structures of classical languages. The third argument joins in to say that the structures of language are in fact the structures of human personality and human society, and that the structures of classical languages have outlived their usefulness. We have changed the way we describe ourselves, and Classics is not good for us any longer.

FOURTH ARGUMENT: THE NATURAL EXTINCTION OF CLASSICS

The mutual reinforcement of the first three arguments creates the fourth, and perhaps most persuasive, argument against classical education. This argument looks at classical education as a social and cultural practice, which, like all such practices, is subject to evolution, change, and possible disappearance. When animal sacrifice, for example, ceased to answer the needs of human beings, human beings stopped slaughtering animals in worship. No single reason can account for the cessation of this or any other cultural practice, and no decisive moment marks its demise.

Classical education is a cultural practice. It began in the Renaissance and developed in response to historical, social, and cultural needs and pressures. At some point—and perhaps the conflict between Wilamowitz and Nietzsche marks the turning—classical education took on a form that did not admit of further development in the direction urged by successive changes in the institutions that sustained it. Now it may be on the verge of becoming extinct. The decisive cultural discontinuity expressed by modernism and confirmed by postmodernism makes it possible to live at last as an educated person without privileging knowledge of Greece and Rome. The revolution against which Newman argued is complete.

To give a complete account of this or any cultural discontinuity is probably impossible, but it is possible to point out some fundamental incompatibilities between our present cultural condition and the two great paradigms of classical education, *Altertumswissenschaft* and liberal arts education. Both paradigms cannot survive the great remapping of our intellectual landscape that has led to the disappearance of objectivity.

The End of Altertumswissenschaft

By "objectivity" I mean the belief or assumption that for any object in the real world there exists a possible set of statements that will constitute a full description of that object. To put it another way, or two other ways: classicists have believed that we can say what is the case about something, or that we can say what we know about something. Both these beliefs now seem to be false.

They seem false because they assume that what we say can somehow be separated from what we say it about, whether we say it about an object or about our mental conception of that object, about a thing or about an idea. Yet as we have seen, this notion of predication, Western philosophy's ancient problem, has come to seem less and less probable to linguists, philosophers, psychologists, and social and literary critics. There seems to be a chasm between word and world, or between language and things, including the users of language. Rather than bridge the chasm with structures of meaning, these thinkers now prefer to leave it unspanned and to devote their attention to the side they occupy, where word and language provide enough to talk about. Ludwig Wittgenstein, at an early stage in his thinking on this issue, pronounced that the world is the totality of facts, not of things.[30] Things, that is, are forever out of reach. Only facts, things about things, can be part of the human world.

In the world of facts, not things, *Altertumswissenschaft* dies. That paradigm depended, we recall, on reconstructing the ancient world in its wholeness, from Attic tragedy to the drainage system of ancient Athens. This reconstruction objectified the ancient world. The world of antiquity became an object represented, or literally re-presented, in language. Powerful, subjective energies and passions might enter into the creation of this world, yet, as Wilamowitz saw it, if those energies, our heart's blood, remained in the final reconstruction, in the revivified ancient world, then the project of *Altertumswissenschaft* had failed.[31]

The problem, we now know, is that the project must fail. Knowledge of the ancient world cannot meet the conditions necessary for this kind of objective reconstruction. The ideal of *Altertumswissenschaft* assumed that what we say about the ancient world could attain a kind of scientific objectivity, and the very name *Altertumswissenschaft*, the "science of antiquity," implies that promise of objectivity. For a moment in history, roughly from F. A. Wolf's legendary matriculation to the death of Wilamowitz, it seemed that statements about the ancient world might have the same kind of truthfulness that statements in science or mathematics have.

Scientific statements do claim a special kind of truthfulness, although many scientists, aware of the problems of predication, would no longer describe them as "objective." It makes better sense to describe scientific truths as "necessary" or "compelling" truths and to distinguish them from the "contingent" truths of art, literature, and other modes of discourse. Daniel Dennett cites a famous question posed by Nicholas Humphrey: "If you were forced to 'consign to oblivion' one of the following masterpieces, which would you choose: Newton's *Principia*, Chaucer's *Canterbury Tales*, Mozart's *Don Giovanni*, or Eiffel's Tower?" Humphrey's answer is,

> I'd have little doubt which it should be: the *Principia* would have to go. How so? Because, of all those works, Newton's was the only one that was *replaceable*. Quite simply: if Newton had not written it, then someone else would—probably within the space of a few years. . . . The *Principia* was a glorious monument to human intellect, the Eiffel Tower was a relatively minor feat of romantic engineering; yet the fact is that while Eiffel did it *his* way, Newton merely did it God's way.[32]

Dennett sees scientific truths in evolutionary terms. They are facts, in Wittgenstein's sense, not things, and they are products of individual responses to cultural forces operating over time, just like works of art; scientific truths, however, have a difference:

> Intuitively, the difference is between discovery and creation, but we now have a better way of seeing it. On the one hand, there is design work that homes in on a best move or forced move which can be seen (in retrospect, at least) to be . . . accessible from many starting points by many different paths; on the other hand, there is design work the excellence of which is much more dependent on exploiting (and amplifying) the many contingencies of history that shape its trajectory.

The best *Altertumswissenschaft* resembles *Don Giovanni* much more than it resembles Newton's *Principia*. Its excellence depends, as Dennett puts it, on making the best of the contingencies of history that create the circumstances of its existence.

First of these contingencies is the author. Scholars create scholarship; they do not discover it. No one but Wilamowitz, with his deep personal commitment to a secular *fides Platonica*, could have written *Platon*. It is as personal and passionate a book as his memoirs.[33] And it is a very different book from, for example, Gregory Vlastos's *Socrates, Ironist and Moral Philosopher*, not because Wilamowitz discovers different truths about Socrates or Plato than Vlastos does, but because each book is the creation of a different sensibility. If Vlastos or Wilamowitz had not written their books, no one else would have. No one else could have.[34]

Although the best *Altertumswissenschaft* is as personal and passionate as poetry, and as much the product of the intersection of historical contingencies and a human creator, scholarship is not the same as poetry. Like every mode of discourse, classical scholarship proceeds according to its own rules. The rules of the game of *Altertumswissenschaft* dictate that statements about the ancient world be both historical and supported by evidence. Historical statements are in principle verifiable; that is, they are statements that could have been verified by the experience of a human witness to the events they describe.[35] "In 431 B.C. war broke out between Athens and Sparta," is an example of a historical statement.

Not all historical statements are true. "An elephant was exhibited on the Acropolis of Athens in 431 B.C.," for example, is a historical but probably false statement; "in 431 B.C. the Persians conquered Sparta" is historical but certainly false. In order to be accepted as true in the game of *Altertumswissenschaft*, a historical statement must be supported by evidence. This evidence consists of other statements about the ancient world. The statements constituting evidence, however, have a special characteristic. They bear some relationship not merely to potential experience of the ancient world (the experience someone could have had looking for an elephant on the Acropolis in 431 B.C., for example), but to our actual present experience of the remains of the ancient world, everything from potsherds to texts in Latin and Greek. If I am going to assert, within the rules of *Altertumswissenschaft*, that an elephant was on the Acropolis in 431 B.C., I must have some present experience that bears on the existence of that elephant in that place and time.

The requirement in the game of *Altertumswissenschaft* that state-ments about the ancient world be both historical and supported by evi-dence does not, however, make such statements necessary, compelling, or "scientific" in the sense that Kepler's laws of planetary motion are sci-entific. To see why statements within the game of *Altertumswissenschaft* are contingent, we must return to the idea of *Altertumswissenschaft* as an objective reconstruction of the ancient world. We can, if we want, think of this reconstruction as an encyclopedia containing a complete descrip-tion of what is known about antiquity.

Such an encyclopedia does exist.[36] It is one of the great monuments of nineteenth- and twentieth-century *Altertumswissenschaft*, and proba-bly as important a document of the human desire for knowledge as the eleventh edition of the *Encyclopedia Britannica*. Well into the twentieth century, new volumes of Pauly-Wissowa, as American classicists usu-ally call the *Real-Enzyclopädie der klassische Altertumswissenschaft*, kept appearing, not only with new articles, but with complete revisions or replacements of earlier entries. A completely new version is now in progress.[37] The encyclopedia of antiquity will never be complete.

Why? Sometimes there are new facts or new pieces of evidence that need to be described and brought into previous descriptions: a new papyrus fragment of Greek poetry, for example, or a new inscription. More often, however, Pauly-Wissowa needs to be rewritten not because our stock of facts has changed, but because we have begun to tell different stories about the ancient world. The physical remains of the ancient world are finite. In theory at least it is possible that someday all the papyrus fragments will have been recovered and edited, all the ancient sites excavated, and all the manuscripts of ancient authors collated and their texts edited. But there is no theoretical limit to the process of giving an account of the ancient world.

The boundless nature of *Altertumswissenschaft* depends on the requirement that statements about the ancient world be supported by evidence. Evidence, remember, is not the physical remains of the ancient world. If it were, then it would be possible to run out of evidence, and so to run out of statements in the game of *Altertumswissenschaft*. Evidence consists of statements about present experience of the physical remains of the ancient world. Present experience must be different for every player in the game of *Altertumswissenschaft*. Because the present experience of every classical scholar is part of *Altertumswissenschaft*, statements in the game are necessarily contingent on the players and as varied and boundless as they are. As long as the game continues, there will be new things to say.

In the 1870s, as *Altertumswissenschaft* was reaching its acme, Nietzsche recognized this connection between a vital philology—his word for *Altertumswissenschaft*—and the experience of the philologist:

> Philology as knowledge of the ancient world cannot, of course, last forever; its material is exhaustible. What cannot be exhausted is the always new adjustment every age makes to the classical world, of measuring ourselves against it. If we set the philologist the task of better understanding *his own* age by means of antiquity, then his task is eternal.—This is the antinomy of philology. *The ancient world* has in fact always been understood only *in terms of the present*—and should *the present* now be understood *in terms of the ancient world*? More

precisely: men have explained the ancient world in terms of their own experience; and from what they have in this way obtained of the classical world, they have *appraised* and evaluated their own experience. Hence *experience* is clearly an absolute prerequisite for a classicist.[38]

The topic continued on his mind, though in a more general form without specific reference to classical philology, ten years later in "We Scholars" from *Beyond Good and Evil*. Although he and Wilamowitz agreed that the personal experience of the classical scholar had a bearing on scholarship, Nietzsche did not share Wilamowitz's confidence that the blood of the scholar's heart could be expelled from the ghosts who had come to life with its aid. Nietzsche was more prescient than his rival in recognizing the potential hazards of an impossible belief in objectivity.

> So deeply and frequently oppressive is the *uncertainty* in scholarly *intuition* that it sometimes becomes a morbid passion to *believe* at any price and a hunger for certainty.[39]

This hunger can no longer be satisfied. *Altertumswissenschaft* is dead, starved by its inevitable failure to attain the objectivity it sought.

The End of Classical Liberal Arts

These are not simply questions for philosophers or cloistered scholars. Shifting epistemologies affect the foundations of private and public life. The replacement of the liberally educated governing classes of Europe and America by bureaucracies in which there is no fact of the matter, no locus of decision, is the political reification of the disappearance of objectivity. Liberal arts education, the second great paradigm of the academic endeavor called Classics, depends on the dream of a different kind of objectivity, not the historical objectivity of *Altertumswissenschaft* but the personal, psychological objectivity of postmedieval European thought. This objectivity, too, has vanished.

Liberal arts education began with the shaping of a governing class, Renaissance princes and courtiers, through the inculcation of tastes, values, and attitudes modeled on classical antiquity. This education drew on fundamental distinctions first made in ancient Greek thought: being versus becoming, mind versus body, and thought versus action. Although Aristotle was not the first to make these distinctions, his account of them in his definition of what he called "First Philosophy" gave them enduring primacy.[40] Liberal arts education, like the ancient philosophical tradition on which it drew, accepted the Aristotelian distinctions and made them the basis of its claim to develop students' minds as entities separate from their bodies, to lead students to an appreciation of the eternal truths of the world of being, and to prepare them to think about things in general, not to act in any particular trade or profession. Classical studies, as Newman put it in "Christianity and Letters," were "the best instruments of mental cultivation, and the best guarantees for intellectual progress," not tools for practical life.

Liberal arts education depended on this idea of "mental cultivation," and on the conviction that each person has a physical component, a body, an intellectual component, a mind, and a spiritual component, a soul, which together create a unique self or personality upon which education operates. The self, as in William Johnson Cory's exhortation to the students of Eton, could become the object of knowledge. It is no coincidence, I think, that liberal arts education had its origin in the humanism of the Renaissance, just at the point when the concept of personality began to be part of the universe of European discourse.

Along with this claim to make the individual self the object of education, liberal arts education depended on the assertion that in the unchanging world of being existed something called human nature. Truths about this human nature formed an object of liberal knowledge, and possession of them constituted a liberally educated person. Knowledge of the self, in this scheme, was also knowledge of universal, unchanging truth.

The best sources for an account of this universal human nature, and the best documents to use in teaching someone about it, were to be found in classical antiquity. Newman, as he laid the foundations of the modern idea of liberal arts, made explicit this association of universal human nature and classical antiquity:

> While the world lasts, will Aristotle's doctrine on these matters last, for he is the oracle of nature and of truth. While we are men, we cannot help, to a great extent, being Aristotelians, for the great Master does but analyze the thoughts, feelings, views, and opinions of human kind. He has told us the meaning of our own words and ideas, before we were born.[41]

Newman's last sentence articulates the belief at the core of liberal arts education that correct knowledge of the self is also knowledge of ideas that are both universal and classical.

Neither the belief in the self as object of education nor the belief in universal human nature as an object of knowledge can survive dissolution of belief in the entity upon which they depend: the self, the conscious, thinking "I" that gives each of us, we have thought, our sense that there is someone at home inside our bodies. Yet that belief in the reality of the Cartesian *ego* has become harder and harder to sustain. For one thing, neurobiology has come closer and closer to demonstrating that emotion, reason, memory, and other functions that we have thought of as mental arise from purely physical structures and physiological operations of the brain and nervous system;[42] for another, the fusion of philosophy, linguistics, psychology, artificial intelligence, and biology called cognitive science has developed a theoretical and experimental model of consciousness that shows how complex mental structures can be produced by physical structures as simple as neurons.[43] Our sense that we are spiritual minds operating in physical bodies is evolving into a sense that each of us is, in Richard Feynman's brilliant description, a recurrent pattern in the dance of atoms.[44]

This newly evolving picture of the individual self entails the disappearance of its collective corollary, belief in unchanging truths of human nature. If our individual consciousnesses are functions of our physical being, then as a group they must be subject to the same evolutionary development that modifies and transforms our species along with all other living things. Statements about a changeless human nature cannot occupy any world of unchanging truths—except, perhaps, for the statement that changeless human nature does not exist! Human nature is and must be part of the biological world in which all things change and evolve.

Modern liberal arts education rested on three pillars: first, the idea of "mental cultivation," predicated on the assumption that mind was essentially different from body; second, the idea of "human nature," an unchanging, universal body of truths about humanity; and third, the notion that it was possible to prepare students to think about things in general without preparing them to think about any single vocational or practical subject. The first two pillars have crumbled. What of the third?

The belief that liberal arts can be defined as those studies that prepare students not for any specific trade or profession, but for generalized problem solving or further professional training has proved the most enduring of the three pillars. It is, after all, close to a simple description of the present state of subjects like Classics in the curricula of colleges and universities: these are the subjects that people do not know what to do with. College and university administrators, if their catalogs are any guide, seem far readier to characterize the liberal arts as nonvocational than to give them explicit epistemological, psychological, or cultural definition.

But important knowledge, in the present state of our culture, tends to be practical knowledge. By "practical" I do not refer to where important knowledge leads, but to where it comes from. The things we know arise from the things we do, from our practices. If, for example, the relationship between mind and body is seen as a purely philosophical problem, it remains insoluble. When it is posed in the context of neurobiological and psychological experimentation and models drawn from practices as varied as computer technology and quantum mechanics, it begins to become tractable.[45]

When basic questions about what it means to be human can be approached by experimentation and computer modeling, it becomes impossible to defend any dichotomy between theory and practice. As John Dewey saw nearly seventy years ago, the evolution of ways of knowing rooted in practice leads inevitably to changes in the way we imagine ourselves to be. Greco-Roman culture's Aristotelian distinction between thought and action, which undergirded the educational concept of liberal arts, can no longer stand.

> Science advances by adopting the instruments and doings of directed practice, and the knowledge thus gained becomes a means of the development of arts which bring nature still further into actual and potential service of human purposes and valuations. The astonishing thing is that in the face of this change wrought in civilization, there still persist the notions about mind and its organs of knowing, together with the inferiority of practice to intellect, which developed in antiquity as the report of a totally different situation.[46]

The belief in liberal arts as studies that equip students with generalized problem-solving skills rather than training for a trade or profession might survive Dewey's criticism if "the instruments and doings of directed practice" simply became part of those subjects. Important knowledge, practical in the sense that it arises from practice, could still be at the center of liberal arts. But knowledge can have another kind of importance. Important knowledge can be understood as the knowledge of important people. Important knowledge is knowledge that leads to power. In American culture at the beginning of the twenty-first century, that knowledge is technological as well as scientific. Our governing class is defined by what it does, not by the way it thinks. The tastes, values, and attitudes of this bureaucratic governing class arise from its practice of governing, from problem solving, and from the practice of particular skills or professions. Those who hope to join the governing class become lawyers, or administrators, or systems analysts. When they do, their exercise of power is more likely to be shaped by legal practices or administrative regulations or technological considerations than by study of Plato, Vergil, Shakespeare, or Emerson. It is no longer the case, as Newman hoped it would be, that "the Philosopher, indeed, and the man of the world differ in their very notion, but the methods, by which they are respectively formed, are pretty much the same."[47]

Developments in philosophy, linguistics, and social criticism have made it impossible to sustain the belief in historical objectivity that undergirded *Altertumswissenschaft*. Developments in neurobiology and cognitive science have made it impossible to believe in the existence of mind and human nature, which liberal arts education claimed as its objects. The twin paradigms of classical education have outlived their usefulness. It is time to put them away. *The books were still upstairs. But reading . . . when had people stopped doing that? The old woman closed her eyes.*

Chapter 4

PROLEGOMENA TO A
PRAGMATIC CLASSICISM

Come, Muse, migrate from Greece and Ionia;
Cross out, please, those immensely overpaid accounts,
That matter of Troy, and Achilles' wrath, and Eneas', Odysseus' wanderings;
Placard "Removed" and "To Let" on the rocks of your snowy Parnassus;

Walt Whitman, "Song of the Exposition"

I may seem to have written a book about the death of classical studies in America. That has not been my intention, nor is that outcome my hope; indeed, in the years since I began the line of thinking that led to this book, increasing numbers of students in American secondary schools have begun to study Latin, and in universities Classics has continued to attract students at all levels and to engage, sometimes in productive ways, with contemporary theory. Outside the academic world, Greeks and Romans (or Greekoids like Xena the Warrior Princess) attract audiences in film, television, and fiction.[1] Yet the trend is so feeble that it can hardly be called upward, especially in higher education. Enrollments in Classics, especially in courses that actually use Greek and Latin, remain hardly visible against the background of American education (above, p. 86, note 1), and knowledge of these two

117

languages, even critics of Classics acknowledge (above, p. 91), is indispensable to understanding Greece and Rome.

Minuscule shifts of numbers or a popular fad for sword-and-sandal movies count for little against structural and historical realities. If classical education has from its beginning depended on social and cultural conditions that have never existed in America and on ideas of historical objectivity and the human personality that are no longer tenable, what alternative remains but to announce its continued, inevitable withering away in this country? What possible place can the study of Greece and Rome have in American education or in America? If the Muse migrates from Greece and Ionia, as Whitman hoped, can her old songs of Troy or Aeneas still make sense?

These are difficult questions, and I cannot claim to have definitive answers for them. Yet it may be possible to begin to imagine an American form of classical education grounded in American personal and social reality as firmly as European classical studies were grounded in the society they served. In this final chapter I hope to sketch some of the characteristics that such an education might have. I do not intend to make very many specific recommendations about curriculum, because what is actually taught, in my experience, always results from a complex and essentially local process in which educational theory is tempered by human personalities, compromise, and tradition. Nor will I offer any complete theory of classical education. This short book aims at provoking a conversation, not solving a problem.

Three features will distinguish an American classical education from its European predecessor. First, American classical education will connect with one essential aspect of its tradition by remembering that it must be a way of becoming human and humane. If Classics cannot help those who practice it to become that, it is worthless. Because it is a way of becoming human, classical education entails a variety of human relationships. Those between teacher and student, or between reader and text, are by no means the simplest. Second, American classical education and American classical studies will modify or reject some European patterns of education and scholarship that alienated American classical studies from the dialogue of American public life in the nineteenth and twentieth centuries. In so doing they will draw on the progressive, democratic strain in the practice of a few American classicists, both those of the present day and their predecessors;[2] at the same time, they will avoid the temptations of some postmodern theories that deny language and literature any possibility of interacting with the human world and make them instruments of power rather than the creators of the powerful. Finally, American Classics will grow out of and respond to the American cultural self, which is indeterminate and various. It will thus respond to Jaeger's provocative challenge by refusing to depend on "the ancient idea of humanity in human culture" (above, p. 44 and n. 2).

A classical education with these characteristics stands a chance of developing a coherent idea of its social function and reordering the conceptual and social structures of classical studies to avoid unnecessary elitism. It may be able to ground itself in reasonable accounts of how language works to construct human consciousness, and it may even be able once again to offer an artificial structure whose purposes will be to explain American civilization and ease the way to its complexities and hard truths, and to encode values and attitudes that temper and strengthen the collective self-awareness of American citizens and prepare them to govern themselves and others (above, p. 5). The four arguments will not go away, but they will become less persuasive because the conclusion to which they lead will no longer strike at the heart of classical studies. Belief in objectivity and a human nature that generates universal cultural truths will no longer be essential to classical scholarship or liberal arts education

BECOMING HUMAN(E)

Calling for a distinctively American classical education does not entail radical separation from some features that defined its European predecessor. Classics is not a distinct academic subject but rather a form of education. Because American classical studies have lost sight of that fact, they have become alienated from the discourse of American public life. American classical studies can heal that alienation only by deliberately aiming to become a form of education: a grammar of civility that encodes, explains, and enacts what it means to be fully human in American society, as Classics once did in Europe. In doing so, American Classics will continue to use Greece and Rome as instruments of education. It will seek to transform the represented experience of these cultures into present experience in American society.[3] It is possible to describe this transformation as three processes, involving both the reconstruction of the past in its totality, as the *Altertumswissenschaft* of Boeckh and Wilamowitz demanded, and also its interpretation in the present. Let us call the processes *representation, presentation,* and *re-presentation.*

First, classical scholarship must achieve a *representation* of the past. Doing so means treating the Greco-Roman past as an object of study by a knowing subject. The vast apparatus of *Altertumswissenschaft*, the grammars, lexicons, editions, indexes, concordances, encyclopedias, books, journals, monographs, reviews, and dissertations, all aim at this representation of antiquity. That which was must be discovered, preserved, and brought before us in its totality as we think it was, as an event from history and as an object of study. It matters and will continue to matter whether *agatha* at Plato, *Apology* 30b 2–4 is subject or predicate, what is the formal structure of recognition scenes in the *Odyssey*, or how we reconstruct the first performance of *Iphigenia at Aulis*.[4]

Second, classical scholarship must achieve a *presentation* of the past. Every understanding of the past exists as part of a continuum of interpretation. All interpretations seek to make the past available for understanding in the present. Not all classical understandings, however, aim at representation of the past, because that aim derives from post-Enlightenment historical consciousness and from the tradition of *Altertumswissenschaft*.[5] Some aim at *presentation* of the past; that is, they put the past before us not as a distanced object of historical understanding but as a present reality, which is entirely part of the same world in which we have our existence.

Examples of presentation can be seen most clearly not in traditional scholarship, but in performance. Nearly every performance of a play, whether by Sophocles, Shakespeare, or Suzan-Lori Parks, attempts to set the play before us as an event on this evening, in this place, now.[6] During the performance the play has no other reality for those who are part of its experience. The audience of Peter Meineck's production of *Agamemnon* in 2004 did not expect to see a *representation* of Aeschylus's play, an objective study of a text that would remain resolutely something apart from their present moment. They expected to see the play itself, *Agamemnon*, then and there, in New York, on a February evening. Performances that objectify a play by seeking to recreate some imagined authentic or original performance often fail their audiences by becoming something they look at rather than something they experience.[7]

Finally, American classical scholarship and American classical liberal education must combine to achieve a *re-presentation* of the past. In this re-presentation will be realized the coming together of classical scholarship and a distinctively American classical and liberal education. Through this unification of the classical paradigms as new, distinctively American forms of *Altertumswissenschaft* and liberal arts, Americans will be able to develop a grammar of our own civility and learn a language in which we can speak our own humanity to one another.

Re-presentation is the act of interpretation through which represented experience becomes present experience. Re-presentation differs from presentation, making that which is interpreted wholly present, in that re-presentation continually reaches out to the irretrievable pastness of what is re-presented. That which is *represented* is entirely past, an object of study. That which is *re-presented* is neither entirely past nor wholly present. The re-presented work carries into the present not only the experience that the work itself conveyed at a particular historical moment, but also the transformations of that experience as the work is interpreted and reinterpreted. Although each experience depends on its historical context and on its place in a continuum of understanding, all understandings exist simultaneously and interact with one another. Thus Dante's experience as a reader of Vergil's *Aeneid* influences the *Divine Comedy*, but equally the *Divine Comedy* becomes part of a tradition of reading and thus influences our understanding as we read Vergil. Our experience of a re-presented work attempts, though the attempt must fail, to include all previous experience of the work.[8]

When, for example, we read Vergil's *Aeneid* not only as a *represented* piece of historical evidence for the Augustan era, and not only as a *presented* narrative of exile and self-discovery immediately before us, but also as a text that calls us to position our reading in a tradition of readings,[9] and from that positioning to create a present meaning for the *Aeneid*, then we have re-presented the *Aeneid*. We have given that poem and its already created meanings a place in our experience. The *Aeneid* becomes more than simply evidence for the past (above, pp. 40-41).

This kind of reading can be described from many points of view: as intertextual reading, as reception-criticism, as new historicism, and no doubt in other ways as well. All of them acknowledge that meaning is something created, not something found. I want to suggest, however, that creating meaning through re-presentation may offer something more than simply a way of reading classical texts or even of interpreting other kinds of evidence from the ancient world. In a larger context, re-presentation may be one way to realize our full humanity. Classical education, furthermore, may be one of the best ways for us to help one another attain that realization.

I am led to this suggestion by the observation that the desire to create meaning seems to be a fundamental part of being human. We do not only want to live in the world. We also want to make sense of it. Through our attempts to construe the world, we face as best we can our tragic situation as grammatical beings in an ungrammatical world (above, p. 101). If this hermeneutical impulse were limited to literary texts and similar artifacts of high culture, it would be interesting to an elite few but could not form the ground of education in a society. A form of education above all has to be a way of becoming human by joining our humanity to that of others; it cannot endure as only a way to set oneself apart from humanity. We have seen that as long as classical education was connected to the society in which it functioned, it made sense; when, as Emerson prophesied and Jaeger saw, it attempted to endure in a society from which it had become disconnected, it ceased to cohere. It became an imitation of what had once made sense. It became radios of twigs and seagull feathers, and waiting for signals that will never come.

Our fundamental human desire to create meaning comes into play not merely when we encounter poems or paintings or music, but even and especially as we come to know another human being. Such encounters can succeed or fail, and success—if that is the right word—in knowing another human being takes many forms. To the extent that human encounters transform themselves into friendship or love, they depend on entering into dialogue with another person. In entering into dialogue we open ourselves to the possibilities that may be there in the other person, in what he or she is, and in otherness and difference; at the same time, we admit to ourselves that this encounter, this dialogue, may change our idea of who we are.[10]

In the most developed form of knowing another person—let us call it love—this dialogue becomes a continual discovery of meaning and a continual transformation of the meanings of both lover and beloved to each other. Each comes to mean something different, and to know something different about the other. In this circumstance, our essential, human desire to know, to understand, and to interpret approaches satisfaction, although because we are human, we can never attain it. In love, as Martin Buber puts it, "Because this person exists, meaninglessness, however hard pressed you are by it, cannot be the real truth."[11] Love is a continual openness to transformation through creation of new meanings.

Some encounters with some texts can be like this. (I am interested here in texts but will suggest in passing that what I say about them may apply to other kinds of artifact.) If we enter into dialogue with a text, move beyond simple wish to know what it states, and open ourselves to its possibilities for meaning, we can transform both ourselves and the text. As the text comes to mean more, so we come to a different, enlarged understanding both of ourselves and of it. We become someone other than what we were before we encountered the text.

Because classical texts have been continuously read and interpreted in European and American education and culture, they offer the best way within those cultures to attain the enlarged understanding of humanity toward which liberal education and humane scholarship can lead. The continuous use of Greece and Rome to parse our civility ensures that the act of *re-presenting* classical civilization will be richer and more filled with possibilities for the creation of meaning than other kinds of interpretation in the humanities.

Here at last is the justification for an American classical education. That American form of education will not simply appeal to tradition, to knowledge for its own sake, or to eternal truths about human culture. It will justify itself by its power to transform experience in the present. A classically educated person continually turns represented experience into present experience. The richer the represented experience, the richer the present experience. Because classical texts exist, because they have existed, and because we have always been engaged in understanding them, our experience of them can be rich indeed. Meaninglessness, however hard pressed we are by it, cannot be the real truth. As both Nietzsche and Wilamowitz knew, and as we in America may yet come to know, classical scholarship and classical education are a transformation of the self, and a work of love.

EUROPEAN MODELS, AMERICAN VERSIONS

In constructing a grammar of civility, a way to transform the self by negotiating it against culture, this new American classical education cannot be simply a transplanted version of European classical education. That project, I have shown, has failed. Different cultures demand different constructions of the self and call for different negotiations of self against culture. American classical education will, however, continue its dialogue with its ancestor by organizing itself around the two great paradigms of classical education: liberal arts and *Altertumswissenschaft*. Through them it will re-present classical education in a new world. With them it will attempt to form the grammar of an American civility.

American Classical Liberal Arts

Education is the process of showing young people how we create meaning in the world. Through this act of understanding a young person gradually learns to negotiate self against culture; that is, to work out and learn to choose among alternative possibilities and manifold ways of being human. To accomplish this educational transformation, it is necessary first to discipline a child's intellect; that is, to shape the child's thought around a *disciplina*, a way of knowing, learning, and teaching. Classical, liberal education is a *disciplina* in this sense, an ordered way of demonstrating the creation of meaning. Hence liberal arts education has to begin in schools. If a child—or better, a young person—does not begin at about the age of twelve or thirteen to form the habits of mind and acquire the base in knowledge that classical, liberal arts education demands, he or she may never do so.

Education in schools after the elementary levels must aim not at preserving the natural curiosity of young children, for doing so creates childish, unfocused adults, but at replacing childish curiosity with adult desire to know and understand. To make this replacement, classical education models the creation of meaning by moving from *representation* to *re-presentation*. A child can be curious about what is represented, but the child's curiosity is satisfied when what is represented becomes an object of his or her own thought. "Did the Romans wear pajamas?" a child may ask.[12] The answer to the question is enough, or it leads to another, similar question. What is re-presented, on the other hand, reveals no answers, only multiple possibilities for meaning. In encountering what is re-presented, older young people conceive a desire to understand. They can satisfy that desire only by entering into open dialogue with what is there; that is, by themselves becoming part of the process of re-presentation. In classical education, classical languages are the instruments through which this move is accomplished.

Because classical education depends on Latin and Greek and mediates meaning through them, it must begin with the most fundamental elements; that is, literally the *elementa*, the sounds of language and the letters that represent them. From the very first stages of classical education, a young American never has the luxury of making the child's imperial assumption that what is unknown must be like what is familiar, and that what he or she is learning is natural, normal, or available by right. The classical world is always strange, and far stranger even than any contemporary culture. This vanished world exists only as the meanings that scholars, students, and teachers struggle to create. In classical education, a student learns gradually to build up meaning out of the elements. With even the simplest Latin sentence, merely answering the question or turning the sentence into English is never enough. *Carmen est breve* (above, p. 93) challenges a student to understand what a *carmen* is, and how it differs from a song. To ask "What *else* could this sentence mean?" is an elementary form of re-presentation.

Thus it is necessary to insist that one challenging feature must distinguish our hypothetical American classical liberal arts education from what happens in most American schools today: classical languages, and the hard fact that after a certain age, it is for most people too late to acquire them easily or become really proficient in them. Classical liberal arts education depends on knowing Latin and Greek. Because American classical education seeks to provide a grammar of the negotiable self in society, classically educated Americans must be able to enter into the negotiations of self in other cultures. There is no other way to do that than through the languages in which the negotiations take place. To the extent that Greco-Roman culture provides the paradigm of that negotiation, classically educated Americans will begin to study Latin or Greek early, and they will learn them well.

It is in the later years of adolescence, however, that conscious negotiation of the self typically begins, and with it the development of social and political consciousness.[13] Experience suggests to me that the later years of American secondary school and the first years of college, roughly from sixteen years of age until twenty, form a single period of psychological development. Teaching high-school juniors has not seemed to me that different, if the artificial constraints and institutional silliness of high school are taken out of the equation, from teaching college sophomores. During these four years, in current terms during the eleventh and twelfth grade and the freshman and sophomore years of college, at least some Americans can be touched by a distinctively American classical liberal arts education. In aiming, as all classical education does, at developing the soul and the citizen, this American classical education will also order itself methodologically. Instead of presenting a student with an à la carte menu of subjects, each with what seems to be an equal claim on his or her intellectual hunger, classical liberal education will model a structure of knowledge. It will begin with close study of language, basic questions in philosophy, and fundamental interpretation of texts, and then spiral outward to large historical and aesthetic questions about the self and culture. If in this respect it comes to resemble the old *trivium* and *quadrivium*, in which grammar, logic, and rhetoric led to higher subjects, it will be because both are deliberately artificial structures designed for a similar function: to ease a student's way to the complexities of culture, of self-understanding, and of civic virtue.

This classical education, which challenges students to construct meaning with an ordered, admittedly artificial structure of knowledge built on a limited framework of information, works against two trends in American education and society at the beginning of the twenty-first century: the so-called knowledge explosion, and the educational world's response to it. On a July afternoon in 2004, an Internet search for the phrase "knowledge explosion" yielded over 6,500 hits. By the time this book is published, there will be more. I performed the search in a remote village in north-central Pennsylvania, in a place that does not have regular mail delivery or reliable radio or television reception, far from libraries, newspapers, and all the traditional ways in which information has reached American citizens. Everything we hear and all our experiences seem to confirm that both the amount of information available to us and the ways in which we can gain access to it are increasing. Sometimes it seems that there is more information than we can use or manage and that there is no way to make sense of all that we can discover.

The educational world has responded to the knowledge explosion by what may be called an analytical, reductionist approach.[14] In higher education the stream of knowledge has been channeled into separate subjects or academic disciplines, each with its own apparatus of knowledge, its departments and schools, professional societies and vocabulary, divided and divided again, until those gathered around one rivulet to drink can scarcely know what kind of thirst draws others to a different trickle.

Secondary education has been slower to channel the flood of knowledge into separate streams, but even there separate subjects divide a student's attention, and curricular reformers constantly call for the addition of more subjects in response to changing conditions in society. Too often the solution to the problem of too much knowledge has been to create more categories of knowledge and to give each a smaller piece of the student's time and attention. Especially in secondary education this reduction of knowledge to separate components shapes pedagogy. At the extreme, knowledge is reduced to bits of information, and students are valued to the extent that they can produce or recognize the appropriate bit of information in response to a prompt. Multiple-choice tests measure the educational worth of a student, and students' performances on these tests measure the worth of teachers and schools.

Small wonder that for many intelligent young people, the secret of success, or all too often of survival, in school is to pretend to be stupider than they are. Education, such students intuitively know, has to be more than a series of bits of information, or separate messages to be transmitted, received, and acknowledged. It is, as we have now seen, the grammar of a language called culture (above, p. 4). A young person challenged by an education that demonstrates the creation of meaning first by encountering the classical world *represented* in its most elementary instantiation, its languages, and then by taking part in *re-presenting* the construction of that world's meanings, will not respond by pretending to be stupider than he or she is. As that student encounters the *Aeneid* or the *Iliad* and transforms the experience represented in those works into his or her present experience, education will become generous, rigorous, difficult, and pleasurable.[15] Some of that pleasure will come from recognizing that classical education presents a coherent body of knowledge, so that the practices formed by the most elementary steps in Latin and Greek remain useful at every step of the journey beyond.

It should be noted that since I understand classical education to be education about the self in culture, I assume that our hypothetical, classically educated young Americans will continue to study mathematics and science. For these students, American classical liberal arts would replace what are now called the humanities or, mistakenly, liberal arts. In high school, the subjects called English and social studies, which as now constituted lack intellectual coherence, seem ripe for replacement. Postsecondary education may have to present classical education as a choice, just as it now offers undergraduate colleges of liberal arts alongside business schools or colleges of education.

The need to frame education in the humanities as an ordered structure of knowledge, as what I have called a grammar of culture, provides one clear reason for framing it as specifically classical education. Limiting the content of education to a well-known, restricted body of cultural objects sets students and teachers alike free to explore fundamental questions about knowledge, humanity, and society. We find this limited, liberating body of culture in Greece and Rome. They have not left us timeless truth or unsurpassed beauty, but they have left us tools that are good to think with, and good to educate our young.

American Altertumswissenschaft

No. Let us finally and reluctantly abandon that useful German word.

American Classical Scholarship

The most urgent tasks now facing American Classical Scholarship are to understand and explain why it exists, and to give an account of what it does in society. Such theoretical grounding as American classical studies has enjoyed has, as I have shown, been derived from essentially European traditions, first from Humanism, then from German Idealism and post-Humboldtian educational theory, and more recently from Marxism, structuralism, and other modern and postmodern theoretical stances. Lacking any firm, culturally grounded theoretical basis like the one that Boeckh and others provided for German classical scholarship, American classical studies has dwindled into an activity at the margins of American education and life. Any claim to some other place must be grounded in a coherent theory of knowledge, language, and history. The distinctively American philosophical traditions arising from Pragmatism may provide a reasonable starting point for this grounding.

An essential adjunct to this theorizing project must be the investigation of what classical studies is, and what it has been. The best classical scholars, including Wilamowitz,[16] have always been aware of the history of their practice and of their position in its evolutionary development, and in recent years that awareness has made the history of classical scholarship one of the few areas of growth in classical studies.[17] There are welcome signs that this project is advancing from recovery of the past to interpretation of it, and that investigations of the history of classical scholarship and its role in education may lead to new understandings of it.[18] The evident influence of Greece and Rome on literature, art, and philosophy, which even the sharpest critics of Classics cannot deny, has also led to a surge in studies of the reception of classical ideas, both by classicists and by those working in other areas.[19]

Study of the history of classical scholarship and classical education suggests an important respect in which a distinctively American classical scholarship will differ from its current form. Classical studies exists at present as one academic discipline among many in American colleges and universities. Progressive or opportunistic classicists sometimes advance the claim that Classics is an interdisciplinary subject, but that assertion simply makes Classics one among a smaller group of academic subjects making the same claim. Classical studies, however, is neither an academic discipline nor an interdisciplinary subject. It constitutes a form of education, and along with theology it was the matrix from which nearly all other humanistic disciplines arose. Both in Europe and in America, Classics was late in becoming an academic discipline, and because it seemed to be something familiar and always present in the universities, it failed to take part in the debates that shaped the character of other academic disciplines as they emerged, as well as in the controversies through which advocates of liberal culture shaped the ideology of modern undergraduate liberal education (above, pp. 81–82). At some level Classics has retained its predisciplinary character to this day.

American classical scholarship, then, can best justify itself by pointing to its character as an education and by emphasizing its processes and their continuity across the span of formal education as much as their results. Those who practice classical scholarship must see themselves as engaged in an enterprise that has closer affinities to the classroom than to the laboratory. Unlike the strictly disciplinary humanities, where a university-based historian and a high-school social-studies teacher may have few points of intellectual contact, professional classicists will construct their field as a unity embracing students and teachers at every level. Advanced researchers, university professors, and secondary teachers will conceive themselves as engaged in different forms of the same practice.

NEGOTIATING THE SELF AGAINST CULTURE

As it rebuilds itself around the American cultural self, American classical education will have to enter into dialogue directly with Greek and Roman cultural selves. It will not be able to organize itself around the old, European idea of the humanities or classical humanism. As Jaeger saw, that idea has never set down roots in this country. In appealing to classical humanism as the justification for classical studies, Jaeger counted on his readers' accepting an idea with roots in the Renaissance and, in the form that Jaeger used, at least as old as Winckelmann and Goethe: that the Greeks, and by extension all classical culture, offer unique paradigms of human cultural excellence, and that in studying them human beings of any and all cultures can come to know unchanging verities about "humanity in human culture." The sense of classical culture as set apart by its enduring, qualitative superiority persists in the construction of Euro-American classical studies at the beginning of the twenty-first century. Despite postmodern assaults, the notion of unsurpassable beauty and eternal meaning dies hard. Consider this description of the Elgin Marbles, and by extension all classical Greek culture, published by an eminent classicist in 1990: "Weathered by time but speaking to us directly: august, authoritative, inimitable, a vision of life fixed forever in forms that seem to have been molded by gods rather than men."[20] Or this: "At the core of the Greek belief system lies the conviction that there are unchanging absolutes in the world, ageless and immune from situation and interpretation, a small but vital body of knowledge that is largely agreed-on and indisputable."[21]

A distinctively American classical studies cannot accept Jaeger's postulate or the purple prose that it spawns, not only because Americans instinctively suspect or reject claims of privilege for any culture, including all too often our own, but also because if there were a single, unchanging best pattern for the individual self in relation to human culture, Americans would not be able to use that knowledge. Americans and the dialogue of American public life depend on the idea that whenever the individual citizen interacts with society, humanity is negotiable. A nation can invent itself by negotiating a constitution, and a Jay Gatsby can negotiate his own public persona and personal history. America is a place where you have to work out who you are. Our founding truths are so far from being self-evident that we must continually struggle to rediscover what they mean and how they mean it.

Thus an American classical education cannot justify itself by claiming access to unchanging truths about human culture, or by asserting whatever authority might come from transmitting those truths. In America, unchanging cultural verities have lost their power. Instead, American Classics will draw its educative power from the idea that the Greeks and classical culture in general offer a continual invitation to explore and renegotiate the self against culture. To negotiate the self against culture is to take part in shared forms of human life and in shared discourse about what it means to be human. It is the hard business of working out how to be the best kind of human one can be, in the context of those shared forms. In these negotiations, facts, values, and interpretations are intertwined. Facts are impossible without values, and values without interpretation; interpretations grow from values, and values depend in turn on facts. This pragmatic holism of values, facts, and interpretations forms the philosophical ground of American thought,[22] and it guarantees that American Classics will never run dry. Nietzsche, we recall, had the insight that so long as Classics was understood as the positivistic re-creation of antiquity that he saw in the *Altertumswissenschaft* of his time, it had to become exhausted in time (above, pp. 36–37). His mistake was to suppose that Romantic nihilism was the only alternative.

In suggesting that American classical education cannot depend on the belief that there are unchanging truths about human culture, I do not mean to reject the idea of human nature or the possibility of making true statements that do not depend on a specific cultural context for their truth. It seems likely that human beings are not blank slates, and that in all times and places human personality and social interactions operate within limits set in part by our genes.[23] All education must acknowledge these limits. Some kinds of statement, also, appear to be true independent of any particular human observer or cultural context. Mathematical propositions, for example, seem to be true by virtue of their conformance to the syntactic rules of the mathematical system within which they are made. It is difficult to believe that a triangle on a Euclidean plane surface in any conceivable universe would not have the sum of its angles equal to 180 degrees.[24] Other kinds of statements must be true by virtue of the rules of natural language, like the proposition that the capital of England is a town.[25]

Classical studies, however, are about human culture, not human nature or analytic propositions. In American culture, few questions are as compelling as those that ask about cultural boundaries of individual thought and action. Do women belong in combat arms of the military? Should homosexuals be permitted to marry one another? Is the achievement gap between black and white students in any way related to racial differences in intelligence? Classical studies can help people to think about questions like these because the self in Greco-Roman culture is very different from either the sincere self created by the Renaissance, the authentic self created by Romanticism, or the psychological self created by modernism.[26] By entering into dialogue with classical ideas of the human self, Americans can deepen their understanding of the possible ways to think about hard questions posed by their cultural situation.

The classical self defines character not as the result of choices made by an autonomous self acting in response to fixed cultural rules, but as a self shaped by actions taken by individuals and by their interaction with others. This classical self is indeterminate, unstable, and almost infinitely negotiable against multiple ideas of what is given by nature.[27] In these respects the ancient self resembles the post-Cartesian self suggested in different ways by contemporary philosophy of mind and post-Kantian ethics, neuroscience, artificial intelligence, and postmodernism, and anticipated in some respects by that quintessential American philosophy, Pragmatism.[28] Ancient thinkers, however, used different tools to attack the problem of *how* to create the cultural self. The Greek and Roman need to create the self by negotiation against culture accounts for the ancient philosophical tradition's emphasis on rationality in the form of competitive argument, language use, and life in society in defining what human beings are by nature. These are modes of shared human life, and by saying that they define what it is to be human, the ancient philosophical tradition declares that the self can be created only by shared forms of human life and shared discourse about what it means to be human. By the same token, modern suspicions of reason, grammatical analysis, and restraints imposed by community often rely on an appeal to the subjective "I," an essentially Cartesian concept of the autonomous self, as sole criterion for judgments of value and norms of conduct.

Although I believe that the ancient tools are very good ones and still useful, I do not want to suggest a simpleminded return to ancient ways of thinking; to do that would be to embrace Jaeger's rejected postulate. But in a society where history and philosophy urge continual negotiation of self against culture, dialogue with Greece and Rome becomes a very good way to think about what it means to be human in society. Indeed, it is tempting to suggest that the capacity of the Greeks and Romans to speak to so many people in so many different cultures arises not because they are exemplars of unchanging truth, but because they can become whatever those cultures need as they negotiate their concept of the self. Greece and Rome can speak to everyone because they are in fact no one at all.

The idea that the self in classical culture is indeterminate and negotiable may seem counterintuitive. Surely in the products of that culture we find personal poetry, biographies, dream narratives, vase painting and sculpture assigned to known artists, and other evidence of fixed and determinate selves. More compelling still: when Americans or Europeans look at Greco-Roman antiquity, we see people very like ourselves. We do not have that sense of otherness that makes the ancient Babylonians or Egyptians forever strangers in our world. Surely our recognition of other selves suggests that they are in fact selves like us, each with a unique, autonomous personal identity, capable of realizing an authentic selfhood and free to do so.

I want to suggest that the apparent identity of Greek and Roman personality with modern, post-Cartesian ideas of the self is in part a construction of the modern observer, analogous to the way we see faces in clouds or rock formations. The fact that words like "mind" and "self" have a shared, public use in our world may lead us to conclude that other minds do in fact exist and conceive themselves in the same way that we do,[29] but it is hard to have the same degree of confidence when the words for what seem to be the same things are as unstable as *mens* or *nous*. "The terms 'personality' and 'self'," Christopher Gill observes, "are modern English terms with no obvious equivalents in ancient poetic or philosophical Greek."[30] Or, I would add, in Latin. Our ability to put ourselves in the place of Pericles or Caesar, Plato or Catullus, and to imagine ourselves thinking their thoughts and feeling their feelings, is one consequence of the historical circumstance that I have called classical education.[31] We seem to know the ancients because Greek and Roman culture are more copiously documented than any other premodern culture, and because they have been part of a tradition of knowing in Europe and America. We know them only because we have made their way of talking about themselves into our own. To argue this case would take another book. Let me outline only two examples of the ancient world's indeterminate cultural self, one from ancient medical and philosophical thought and one from the earliest Greek poetry.

Because it sets out to heal the sick human body, medicine would seem to require knowledge of what that body is and how it works. Further, it would seem that everyone, physicians and patients alike, would have to agree on that knowledge and share at least a general idea of what constituted human health; otherwise, how could anyone recognize a good physician or a good therapy? Yet in Greco-Roman medicine, competing ideas of human anatomy and physiology vied for supremacy, just as their adherents vied for patients and professional stature. Dogmatists, Empiricists, Methodists, and other schools, each with its own idea of the functioning of the human body, engaged in continual negotiation and renegotiation of human physical nature.[32]

In the same way, when philosophers and their schools came to think about the self in culture, they found no agreement about the nature of the self or about the limits of human nature. It was thus easy for them to see the analogy between medicine and the branch of philosophy called ethics. As Aristotle put it, "We aim not to know what courage is but to be courageous, not to know what justice is but to be just, just as we aim to be healthy rather than to know what health is, and to be in a good condition rather than to know what good condition is."[33] For Aristotle, the ethical self depends on actions, not on agreed definitions of human virtues. Virtue grows from practice, not from knowledge of unchanging truths about human nature or human culture.[34] When Epicureans, Stoics, Cynics, and other philosophers came to think in Aristotle's wake about difficult questions of the kind posed above (p. 133), they also first had to negotiate an idea of the human self in culture. Although both Stoics and Epicureans, as well as other schools, recognized the existence of a few unchanging truths about human nature, they also believed that, as Martha Nussbaum puts it, "existing desires, intuitions, and preferences are socially formed and far from reliable."[35] We Americans, too, live in a world where what we want, what we instinctively believe, and what we choose for ourselves open themselves to questioning from the society in which they find expression. Awareness of ways in which the classical world accepted the invitation to negotiate the self against culture may help us think our way through this world and make its uncertainties less threatening.

In the Homeric poems, my second example of the negotiable ancient self, characters define themselves as moral and ethical agents not by referring to externally authorized moral codes or to internalized virtues, but instead by negotiating the self and its responsibilities against the thoughts and actions of others. When Agamemnon, for example, wants to acknowledge in front of the Achaean army that he was wrong to take the woman Briseis, Achilles's prize of honor, for himself, he does not frame his responsibility in terms of personal guilt or sin. Instead, he presents it as the result of external, divine forces:

> This is the word the Achaians have spoken often against me
> and found fault with me in it, yet I am not responsible
> but Zeus is, and Destiny, and Erinys the mist-walking
> who in assembly caught my heart in the savage delusion
> on that day I myself stripped from him the prize of Achilleus.[36]

Agamemnon locates his ethical responsibility in the space between the collective reproaches of the Achaeans and divine forces that are beyond his control. As Oliver Taplin observes, our assessment of his character "is closely bound up with his roles and relationships."[37] What his ethical responsibility is depends on his negotiation of his self against these human and divine forces.[38]

To a post-Homeric age, Helen of Troy was the person who entered into an adulterous liaison with Paris and so caused the Trojan War.[39] In the *Iliad*, however, her responsibility takes on a different cast. As they gaze out from the wall of Troy over the opposing Greek forces, King Priam calls her to sit beside him and says, "You are not responsible, indeed I tell you the gods are responsible."[40] Later, when Aphrodite has ordered her to come to bed with Paris, Helen recognizes the goddess and refuses:

> Not I. I am not going to him. It would be too shameful.
> I will not serve his bed, since the Trojan women hereafter
> would laugh at me, all, and my heart even now is confused with
> sorrows.[41]

An autonomous moral agent (or a person who thought of herself as such) might speak of feeling ashamed at returning to the bed of a warrior who has just come off second best in a contest with her former husband. She might object that to do so would be wrong because it would betray her sense of self or would go against norms set by divine sanction or human nature. Helen, however, shapes her response against the reactions of others, the Trojan women whose reproaches she envisions. Like Agamemnon, she negotiates her self and its obligations against the society in which those obligations are enacted.

One way to read the *Iliad*, in fact, is to see it as an extended attempt to show how human beings establish their cultural selves between the poles of other people's responses to their actions on the one hand and, on the other, the hard facts of human nature, especially human mortality. In Book Twelve the warrior Sarpedon, leader of the Lycian contingent of the Trojans' allies, addresses his lieutenant, Glaukos:

> Glaukos, why is it you and I are honored before others
> with pride of place, the choice meats and the filled wine cups
> in Lykia, and all men look on us as if we were immortals,
> and we are appointed a great piece of land by the banks of Xanthos,
> good land, orchard and vineyard, and ploughland for the planting of
> wheat?
> Therefore it is our duty in the forefront of the Lykians
> to take our stand, and bear our part of the blazing of battle,
> so that a man of the close-armoured Lykians may say of us:
> "Indeed, those are no ignoble men who are lords of Lykia,
> these kings of ours, who feed upon the fat sheep appointed
> and drink the exquisite sweet wine, since indeed there is strength

of valour in them, since they fight in the forefront of the Lykians."
Man, supposing you and I, escaping this battle,
would be able to live on forever, ageless, immortal,
so neither would I myself go on fighting in the foremost
nor would I urge you into the fighting where men win glory.
But now, seeing that the spirits of death stand close about us
in their thousands, no man can turn aside nor escape them,
let us go on and win glory for ourselves, or yield it to others.[42]

Sarpedon finds his duty as a war leader in the space between the Lycians' response to him, their reward of social position and their praise, and the hard fact of human mortality. There is no contradiction between his assertion that he and Glaukos fight because they will receive rewards in Lycia and his final declaration that he fights because death is inevitable. Sarpedon negotiates his cultural self, who he is in Lycia, by balancing the claims of human nature against the responses of his fellow citizens to his actions.

Agamemnon, Helen, and Sarpedon, each in a different way, illustrate the culturally negotiable, indeterminate ancient self around which American classical education can form a grammar of civility for an America in which the self is similarly indeterminate. That classical self permits many conclusions to be drawn by those who engage with it; in fact, the very conception of Classics that, I have argued, does not fit American reality originated in just such an engagement. The old idea that the Greeks, and by extension all classical culture, offer unique paradigms of human cultural excellence and unchanging verities about "humanity in human culture" can be traced to a dialogue with the classical self.

Classical humanism, the ground of traditional classical education, grew from the Renaissance discovery and development of the individual, autonomous self.[43] The works of Humanists like Petrarch or Montaigne show that this discovery happened through dialogue with the indeterminate selves of Greco-Roman antiquity. Through its engagement with the voices of classical literature, the Renaissance constructed the modern self, which relates itself to what it knows in the world as knowing subject to known object, and thus created the idea of objectivity that shaped modern science and all that depends on it, including modern education. Let me give one example.

For Michel de Montaigne, his *Essays* had no other subject than their author.[44] When he retired from public life in 1570 to, as he put it, "pass in the company of the learned Virgins what little shall yet remain of his allotted time now more than half run out,"[45] he installed himself in a tower surrounded by five tiers of books, most of them editions of Greek and Roman authors. Three windows gave a panoramic view of the world beyond. Montaigne's almost Borgesian tower provides an apt image for the author as he orients himself in his world against the embracing background of ancient thought. He measured himself against Plutarch and Appian and Socrates and, often, found himself wanting: "If I happen, as I often do, to come across in the good authors those same subjects I have attempted to treat—as in Plutarch I have just this very moment come across his discourse on the power of imagination—seeing myself so weak and puny, so heavy and sluggish, in comparison with those men, I hold myself in disdain." At the same time, the endorsement of antiquity served as a powerful affirmation of Montaigne's own selfhood: "Still I am pleased at this, that my opinions have the honor of often coinciding with theirs, and that at least I go the same way, though far behind them, saying 'How true!'"[46] For Montaigne, education could be seen as a deliberate imitation of antiquity. It was not a matter of absorbing knowledge about Greece and Rome, but rather of approximating the condition of the ancient exemplars through one's own disciplined thought and action; that is, to be educated meant acquiring a classical grammar in order to speak the language of civility: "For if he [the pupil] embraces Xenophon's and Plato's opinions by his own reasoning, they will no longer be theirs, they will be his. He who follows another follows nothing."[47]

An American classical education will engage in a similar dialogue with the Protean selves of ancient Greece and Rome, although its results may be a very different understanding of the self from that of classical humanism. This American dialogue will not aim at discovery of objective truth and unchanging perfection. Instead, it will seek to reveal alternative possibilities and manifold ways of being human, and it will illuminate the pathways by which these alternatives have been realized and the negotiations along the way between what is natural and given and what is human and imagined. Like some early dialogues of Plato, America's dialogue with the ancient world will not reach a conclusion; instead, it will always remain open to multiple constructions and further evolution. It will answer Jaeger by continually inventing and reinventing a new classicism, American and pragmatic rather than European and humane.

The continued presence and relevance of Greco-Roman antiquity in European and American education, then, may be due less to the stable truths and unchanging perfection of ancient culture than to its essential instability and lack of definition. The Greeks, to take them by metonymy for the whole of classical antiquity, may have been able to speak to everyone, including many Americans, because they are in fact no one at all. These Protean Greeks, who take their character from the desires of those who study them, and their equally indeterminate Roman peers, along with all the peoples from Britain to Afghanistan whose cultures felt their imprint and interacted with them, will provide one focus of American classical education.

Education cannot, however, grow entirely from the need to clarify individual knowledge of the self; indeed, an exclusive concentration on what education does for individual students, or for that matter to individual teachers, disconnects education from society and makes it likely that both individuals and the society they form will be dysfunctional. Any education must take account of the society within which it functions and of its effects on that society. In classical terms, education must ask not only what kind of soul it forms but also what kind of citizen.

An American classical education at the beginning of the twenty-first century thus needs to take account of the political and social realities that transformed our nation during the last decades of the twentieth. Two stand out. First, we are now a nation marked, as the classical world sometimes was, by vast inequalities of wealth. When I began teaching in 1969, I was able to tell students that the gap between rich and poor was far wider in ancient Rome than in modern America, and that no one in the modern world was as rich as Marcus Crassus, who once proclaimed that no one deserved to be called rich unless he could maintain an army at his own expense. Several years ago I realized that I could no longer make that statement. According to Plutarch, during his consulship Crassus sacrificed a tenth of his property to Hercules, put on a banquet for all the Roman people, gave every Roman enough to live on for three months, and still had a net worth of 7,100 talents.[48] If we assume that the talents in question are Attic talents of 60 minae, and that a mina equals 100 denarii, then we can calculate the approximate value of a talent based on the value of labor, since a denarius, we know, could purchase a day's labor, or perhaps a bit more, in the first century B.C.[49] All attempts to give a value for denominations of ancient coin are approximate, but we will not be far wrong if we say that a denarius had approximately the purchasing power of fifty dollars in 2003. If so, a talent amounts to approximately $300,000, and Crassus's 7,100 talents make a very respectable fortune, rather over two billion dollars ($2,130,000,000, to be exact—almost exactly what Ted Turner is said to be worth). In September 2003, Bill Gates's net worth was estimated to be in excess of 34 billion dollars.

We are also, as I write these words, engaged in occupying and reconstructing the governments of two countries.[50] We have become an imperial republic, although we prefer to avoid those classical terms. Yet our leaders, at least in their public discourse, avoid any acknowledgement of the moral complexities and potential tragedies of this new role. Here I recall the morning of September 11, 2001. A network systems administrator, whose fundamental education was in Classics, sat in my office, and we talked as we watched the Twin Towers collapse on the tiny screen of my computer. "The powerful thing about being a classicist," he said, "is that we've already seen the world come to an end. More than once." We reached for Augustine's *City of God*. That book is Augustine's response to the sack of Rome by Alaric's Visigoths in A.D. 410. Alaric's raiders left Rome almost as quickly as they arrived, and to many observers it may have seemed as though Rome and her empire were hardly damaged. Even from far away in North Africa, though, Augustine could see that things would never be the same again. In 2001, looking back in hindsight, my friend and I could see that it was Augustine, that suicide bomber attacking the Roman world's soul, not Alaric, who was bringing down the empire in the early fifth century. Just for a moment Augustine was the lever that we needed to open our thinking to the complexities and possible resonances of the events of that September day.[51] In the next few days and weeks we looked for a sign that our political leaders knew where those old tools were, or newer ones that might work as well, but we did not find it.

Although I single out expanding inequality and burgeoning empire as the two most salient features of current American political reality, I do not mean to suggest that American classical education must build itself around those and only those two. Other analyses are and will become possible, but classical education must continually be reaching an understanding of what present society is. It must also be grounded in recognition that thinking about and with Greco-Roman antiquity does not simplify our thought about the present. The Greeks and Romans do not present us with simple, unchanging paradigms of civic virtue and political verity, any more than they present us with exemplars of an unchanging, autonomous human self.[52]

EPILOGUE

Historical self-consciousness, awareness of education at all levels, and hermeneutic foundations cannot be the whole of classical scholarship or classical education. Those activities will remain, as they have been since Wolf, founded on the philological and historical study of the Greco-Roman world. Careful, painstaking thought and study will continue to be needed at every level of American classical studies. Because, however, American classical scholarship will grow out of and respond to American personal and social realities, even the most advanced and technical research will take on a different character from that of its

European ancestor. As it recognizes the destabilization both of the fixed text that has been the object of its study and of the knowing subject, it will seek less to re-create an objective, ideal ancient world and more to create that world anew and to make it active in the world of the present, and especially in the education of the young.[53]

American Classics can become the type of intellectual praxis, a best way to think about the self in action and to educate American citizens in the negotiations of culture. If it does, then the four arguments (above, chapter 3) will be weakened. Because such an education will be fully engaged with society as well as fully conscious of the relations between its practice and its social function, it will be both useful and valuable. It may not be able to avoid the second argument's charge of elitism entirely, because it will continue to ground itself in the study of classical languages. Yet our own history shows that Classics and classical education can be a productive focus of social tensions and controversy and a good tool with which to think about such matters. A socially engaged American Classics will engage its critics and their ideas, and through that engagement it will respond to criticisms of its inevitable elitism. Because an American Classics will depend on an idea of the negotiable self, it will be aware of the way in which grammar and the structures of language shape the self, and so the third argument will be co-opted as part of what Classics is and does. Finally, because classical education will have refounded itself in a new world and remade itself without its old notions of objective reconstruction of the past or unchanging human nature, the fourth argument too will totter and fall.

Many will object—and it would be hard to argue against them—that the odds against any of this happening seem formidable. *Altertumswissenschaft* and liberal arts shaped the modern American university, and universities in turn have shaped American educational life. Revolution or even radical reform in institutions so embedded in society seems unlikely. Transforming them through internal processes produces only incremental change after interminable delay. How can institutions so complex, influential, and deeply planted in American life change to give us a new kind of education, and the institutions to support it? A distinctively American classical education seems at best a distant hope.

Radical transformation has happened before in American higher education, and it did not take long. In the half century between the Civil War and World War I, theorists and visionary executives like Daniel Coit Gilman and M. Carey Thomas, academic leaders like William Rainey Harper, and philanthropists like Leland Stanford created a new kind of educational institution and a new kind of education to inhabit it: the modern research university. It did not take many of them to do it. If American classicists can develop a convincing account of what they do, why they do it, and what value their activities have in American society, the odds will still be long. But we will not be without hope, without love, or without our hearts' blood to make the ghosts speak.

NOTES

Chapter 1

1   These are real titles. They belong to papers delivered at recent annual meetings of the American Philological Association.

2   Brian, *Einstein, A Life*, 129.

3   Baring-Gould, *The Annotated Sherlock Holmes*, 1:154.

4   The great German classical scholar Ulrich von Wilamowitz-Moellendorff reportedly thought and dreamed in ancient Greek.

5   My partition of classical education between liberal arts education and *Altertumswissenschaft* tracks, roughly, Bruce Kimball's distinction between orators and philosophers (*Orators and Philosophers*), and what Gerald Graff (*Professing Literature*, 3) calls "the union of Arnoldian humanism and scientific research."

6   McInerny "Beyond the Liberal Arts."

7   For Vittorino, see Woodward, *Vittorini da Feltre and Other Humanist Educators*; Giraud, "Victorin de Feltre (1378–1447?)."

8   Long before Dr. Arnold introduced the cult of games at Rugby, physical exercise was a staple of Renaissance classical education; e.g. Pier Paolo Vergerio, *De Ingenuis Moribus* 55, in Kallendorf, *Humanist Educational Treatises*, 66–69.

9   Quoted in Morris, *The Oxford Book of Oxford*, 31. On the medieval university as professional school in the service of society's governing classes, see Ruegg, "The University: Product and Shaper of Society."

10 Grafton and Jardine, *From Humanism to the Humanities*, xii. For the modern debate on the political stance of Renaissance humanism, see Bushnell, *A Culture of Teaching*, 10–22.

11 V. H. H. Green, *A History of Oxford University*, 49–50.

12 Locke's criticism of classical education goes deeper than his utilitarian remarks in *Some Thoughts Concerning Education*, 217; for a view of it in the context of his political philosophy, see Pangle and Pangle, *The Learning of Liberty*, 54–72.

13 Clarke, *Classical Education in Britain*, 34–60. Outside England, education could take on a different socio-economic complexion; Scottish universities, for example, reflected that nation's less rigid class structure and cosmopolitan ties with Europe.

14 Darwin and Huxley, *Autobiographies*, 12; of his years at Cambridge, Darwin wrote, "my time was wasted" (ibid., 32).

15 E.g. by Frederic Henry Hedge in an address to Harvard alumni; Hofstadter and Smith, *American Higher Education*, 563.

16 The best modern edition is Ker, *John Henry Newman*.

17 Ker, *Newman*, 5.

18 Pattison, *The Great Dissent*.

19 "Because he appears only to be talking about knowledge, its different forms and rankings, with theology at the top, it is easy to see why discussions of a university that take the *Idea* as a starting point fail to notice how much Newman takes for granted" (Rothblatt, *The Modern University and its Discontents*, 18). Rothblatt goes on to suggest that what Newman takes for granted is "humanism;" that is, Classics.

20 Ker, *Newman*, 221.

21 Ibid., 219.

22 Bloom, *The Closing of the American Mind*, Paglia; "Junk Bonds and Corporate Raiders"; and from a somewhat different point of view Emberly and Newell, *Bankrupt Education*. Also Hanson and Heath, *Who Killed Homer?*; see in addition Heath, "More Quarreling in the Muses' Birdcage," followed by Peter Green, "Mandarins and Iconoclasts," and Hanson and Heath, "The Good, the Bad, and the Ugly."

23 The event was legendary as early as Nietzsche; see Arrowsmith, "Nietzsche," 281.

24 Grafton, Most, and Zetzel, *F. A. Wolf, Prolegomena to Homer*.

25 Kenney, *The Classical Text*, 98 n. 1; Schröder, "*Philologiae studiosus.*"

26 There had been lecturers in humanity, or Latin style, since the foundation of Corpus Christi College in 1517, but their aims and objects were far different from those of a modern professor; Clarke, *Classical Education*, 22–33.

27 Clarke, *Classical Education*, 102–3.

28 On this *Totalitätsideal*, see de Grummond, *An Encyclopedia of the History of Classical Archaeology*, s.v.

29 *Higher Schools and Universities in Germany* (1882), 155, quoted in Clarke, *Classical Education*, 173. Arnold's identification of the humanities with the study of Greek and Roman antiquity has often been overlooked; see Proctor, *Defining the Humanities*, 104–5, and Baker, "The Victorian Chronology of Our Liberal Education."

30 Pfeiffer, *History of Classical Scholarship from the Beginnings to the End of the Hellenistic Age*, 87–104.

31 Grafton, *Joseph Scaliger*.

32 On Winckelmann's influence see Potts, *Flesh and the Ideal*, 222–53. The history of classical scholarship has become an important area of specialization within the history of ideas; from an enormous bibliography see Pfeiffer, *History*, vols. 1 and 2, and Wilamowitz-Moellendorff, *History of Classical Scholarship*. For further bibliography see Calder and Kramer, *An Introductory Bibliography to the History of Classical Scholarship*.

33 Boeckh, *Enzyklopaedie und Methodologie der philologischen Wissenschaften*; Pritchard, *On Interpretation and Criticism*.

34 Hegel, "On Classical Studies," in Simpson, *German Aesthetic and Literary Criticism*, 202–4.

35 Kimmerle, *F. D. E. Schleiermacher, Hermeneutics*.

36 *Die Erkenntniss des Erkannten*; Boeckh, *Enzyklopaedie*, 256.

37 Boeckh, *Enzyklopaedie*, 260.

38 E.g. Hirsch, *Validity in Interpretation*, 245 on the relation between Boeckh and Gadamer's *Wahrheit und Methode* (1960), which Hirsch calls "the most substantial treatise on hermeneutic theory that has come from Germany in this century." Gadamer was trained as a classical philologist.

39 Lloyd-Jones, *Blood for the Ghosts*, 61–75.

40 Grafton, Most, and Zetzel, *F. A. Wolf*, 18–26; on Eichhorn, see also Bietenholz, *Historia and Fabula*, 258–69, and Balfour, *The Rhetoric of Romantic Prophecy*, 106–26.

41 Schelling, *On University Studies*, 40.

42 Dennett, *Darwin's Dangerous Idea*, 136.

43 Bursian, *Geschichte der classischen Philologie in Deutschland*, 2:665–705.

44 Most, "One Hundred Years of Fractiousness."

45 Yale granted Ph.D.s as early as 1861, but the work required there and else-where before the founding of Johns Hopkins hardly qualifies as substantial; see Calder, "The Refugee Classical Scholars in the USA," 155.

46 Briggs, *The Letters of Basil Lanneau Gildersleeve*, 5 and 121, n. 3; on the importance of Johns Hopkins as a pattern for American graduate schools in the humanities as well as the sciences, see Graff, *Professing*, 56–59.

47 On the development of American higher education, see Veysey, *The Emergence of the American University*; Kimball, *Orators*; and Marsden, *The Soul of the American University*.

48 Gutmann, *Democratic Education*, 36.

49 MacIntyre, *After Virtue*, 18.

50 Ker, *Newman*, 154.

51 Fallows, "When George Meets John."

52 On the transition from Renaissance governor to modern manager, see Proctor, *Humanities*, 128–34.

53 See for example Plato, *Meno* 97a ff.

54 Briggs, *Letters*, 120; see also Calder, "Refugee," 156–57.

55 In my account of the Nietzsche-Wilamowitz quarrel I follow Calder, "The Wilamowitz-Nietzsche Struggle," supplemented by Mansfeld, "The Wilamowitz-Nietzsche Struggle."

56 See the comments of Calder, "Wilamowitz," 235–36.

57 See the judicious assessment of Lloyd-Jones, *Blood*, 171–72.

58 Calder, "Wilamowitz," 217–18.

59 *Zukunftsphilologie! eine erwiderung auf Friedrich Nietzsches ord. professors der classischen philologie zu Basel "geburt der tragödie" von Ulrich von Wilamowitz-Moellendorff Dr. Phil.*, translated as Wilamowitz, "Future Philology!"

60 Calder, "Ecce Homo," demonstrates this for Wilamowitz.

61 Henrichs, "The Last of the Detractors."

62 Calder, "Wilamowitz," 251.

63 Nietzsche, *The Birth of Tragedy and the Case of Wagner*, 95.

64 Translated by Arrowsmith, "Nietzsche."

65 Ibid., 282–83.

66 *Die Aufgabe derselben ist freilich nur ein Ideal, welches nie völlig erreicht werden kann, indem es unmöglich ist alle Einzelheiten zu einer Totalanschauung*

zu verbinden; aber es muss wenigstens das Bestreben dahin gehen und die Aufgabe darf nie aus den Augen gelassen werden, Boeckh, *Enzyklopaedie,* 57.

67 Boeckh anticipated this partitioning of *Altertumswissenschaft*: "But even if every scholarly investigator apprehends the truth only one-sidedly and piecemeal, his perception advances the development of science (*Wissenschaft*), and through it gradually there develops a basic body of assured knowledge to which logical, that is methodical principles belong; and in accord with these it becomes possible to distinguish the degree of truth and certainty" (Boeckh, *Enzyklopaedie* = Pritchard, *Interpretation,* 164).

68 Wilamowitz, *Einleitung in die griechische Tragödie,* 257.

69 Calder, "Wilamowitz," 252.

70 Calder, "Ecce Homo."

71 Galinsky. "The *Aeneid* as a Guide to Life," 161.

72 On discussion provoked by this statement, see Rabinowitz and Richlin, *Feminist Theory and the Classics,* 4.

73 Wilamowitz, *History,* 1.

74 The allusion is to Cato the Elder as quoted by Quintilian, *Inst.* 12.1,1.

Chapter 2

1 On Jaeger, see Calder, *Werner Jaeger Reconsidered.*

2 "Without the continuing prestige of the ancient idea of humanity in human culture, classical scholarship is just a waste of time. Whoever does not see this ought to come to America and let himself learn from the way classical studies have developed there." (*Ohne die dauernde Geltung der antiken Idee des Menschen in der menschlichen Kultur schwebt die klassische Altertums-wissenschaft in der Luft. Wer dies nicht sieht, der sollte nach Amerika kommen und sich vom Gang der Entwicklung der klassischen Studien dort belehren lassen;* Jaeger, *Scripta,* 1:xxvi.)

3 White, "Werner Jaeger's 'Third Humanism' and the Crisis of Conservative Cultural Politics in Weimar Germany," 271–73.

4 Cremin, *American Education,* 13.

5 Ibid., 177.

6 Ibid., 182.

7 Kimball, *Orators,* 103.

8 Cremin, *American Education,* 221 and 238.

9 William Livingston, *A Letter to the Right Reverend Father in God, John, Lord Bishop of Landaff* (New York, 1768), 23–24, quoted in Reinhold, *Classica Americana,* 63.

10 Locke, *Some Thoughts Concerning Education*, 217; above, 9.

11 Reinhold, *Classica Americana*, 57.

12 Locke, *Some Thoughts*, 217; above, 10.

13 Cremin, *American Education*, 380.

14 Woody, *Early Quaker Education in America*, 26–40.

15 The Proposals are most easily found in Franklin, *Benjamin Franklin: Writings*, 323–44; for the *Constitutions*, see Woody, *Educational Views of Benjamin Franklin*, 182–91.

16 On Hutcheson, see Cremin, *American Education*, 463–64.

17 *Observations Relative to the Intentions of the Original Founders of the Academy in Philadelphia* (1789); Woody, *Educational Views*, 193.

18 Woody, *Educational Views*, 182.

19 Ibid., 173.

20 No provision is made for them in his *Idea of the English School* (1751); Franklin, *Franklin*, 348–54.

21 *Observations Relative to the Intentions of the Original Founders of the Academy in Philadelphia* (1789), quoted in Woody, *Educational Views*, 204.

22 Woody, *Early Quakers*, 71–72.

23 Quoted in Reinhold, *Classica Americana*, 127.

24 *American Museum*, June 1789, quoted in Reinhold, *Classica Americana*, 129.

25 Quoted in Reinhold, *Classica Americana*, 124.

26 Clark, *Thomas Paine*, civ; Conway, *The Writings of Thomas Paine*, 1:252–53.

27 On the Enlightenment's relationship to classical antiquity, see Gay, *The Enlightenment*, 31–203.

28 For the correspondence, see Cappon, *The Adams-Jefferson Letters* and Ford, "Thomas Jefferson and John Adams on the Classics."

29 Reinhold, *Classica Americana*, 131.

30 Hofstadter and Smith, *American Higher Education*, 156.

31 Letter to Isaac Tiffany, quoted in Reinhold, *Classica Americana*, 108.

32 Bushnell, *A Culture of Teaching*, 23–72.

33 Ong, "Latin Language Study as a Renaissance Puberty Rite."

34 Letter to the Reverend James Muir, Aug. 24, 1791, in Butterfield, *Letters of Benjamin Rush*, 1:604–7.

35 Reinhold, *Classica Americana*, 181.

36 Ibid., 181.

37 Hallett, "Writing as an American in Classical Scholarship," 137.

38 Tocqueville, *Democracy in America*, 317.

39 Ibid., 318.

40 *Life of Emerson*, quoted in Emerson, *Nature*, 415.

41 Emerson, *Collected Works*, 70.

42 According to Oliver Wendell Holmes, quoted in Emerson, *Nature*, 415.

43 Emerson, *Collected Works*, 67.

44 Ibid., 56.

45 Richardson, *Emerson: The Mind on Fire*, 52.

46 Emerson, *Collected Works*, 58.

47 Ibid., 64.

48 Remini, *Andrew Jackson and the Course of American Democracy*, 79.

49 Ibid., 400.

50 Quoted in Remini, *Andrew Jackson*, 79; see also Bentinck-Smith, *The Harvard Book*, 364–67.

51 Hofstadter and Smith, *American Higher Education*, 293.

52 Honeywell, *The Educational Work of Thomas Jefferson*, 251, quoted in Pangle and Pangle, *Liberty*, 161.

53 Pangle and Pangle, *Liberty*, 167.

54 Hofstadter and Smith, *Higher Education*, 176. Emphasis in original.

55 Ibid., 275

56 Ibid., 285.

57 Lanham, *The Electronic Word*, 101–2.

58 Hofstadter and Smith, *Higher Education*, 277. Emphasis in original.

59 Ibid., 289.

60 Ibid., 289.

61 For an example, see Van Sickle, "Towards Interculturalism in Class."

62 Hofstadter and Smith, *Higher Education*, 289.

63 Veysey, *Emergence*, 180–251.

64 Hofstadter and Smith, *Higher Education*, 289.

65 Ibid., 289.

66 Ibid., 290.

67 Ibid., 288.

68 Ibid., 290.

69 On Lincoln as exegete, see Wills, *Lincoln at Gettysburg*.

70 Hofstadter and Smith, *Higher Education*, 486.

71 Emerson, *Collected Works*, 67.

72 Hofstadter and Smith, *Higher Education*, 195.

73 Santayana, *Character and Opinion in the United States*, 141.

74 Veysey, *Emergence*, 311, echoed by Calder, "Classical Scholarship in the United States," xxi.

75 See in general Winterer, *The Culture of Classicism*; Marchand, *Down from Olympus*.

76 Among the other eastward pioneers were George Ticknor (1791–1871), Edward Everett (1794–1865), and Joseph Green Cogswell (1786–1871); see Diehl, *Americans and German Scholarship*.

77 Hofstadter and Smith, *Higher Education*, 264.

78 Emerson, *Collected Works*, 58.

79 Hofstadter and Smith, *Higher Education*, 274.

80 Even as late as 1880 Basil Gildersleeve found British Universities and scholars wanting in comparison with German; see Briggs, *Letters*, 42–45.

81 See Briggs, *Biographical Dictionary of North American Classicists*, for the lives of scholars mentioned in this paragraph.

82 Calder, *Classical Scholarship*, xxviii. M. Carey Thomas's Ph.D. was awarded by the University of Zurich, but only after she had completed most of the work for the degree at Leipzig and Göttingen, neither of which would award a doctorate to a woman; Horowitz, *The Power and Passion of M. Carey Thomas*, 145–65.

83 Pearcy, "Aristophanes in Philadelphia."

84 Veysey, *Emergence*, 96.

85 Ibid., 264–68.

86 Gildersleeve, "The Agamemnon at Oxford."

87 Winterer, *Classicism*, 152–57.

88 Briggs, *Letters*, 70.

89 Among many examples see especially the indispensable and encyclopedic database of Broughton, *Magistrates of the Roman Republic*, the "Harvard Servius" (Rand et al., *Servianorum in Vergilii Carmina*, on which see Fraenkel, "Review of Servianorum"), and Pease's great commentary on *Aeneid* Book 4 (*Publi Vergili Maronis Aeneidos*).

90 Americans conducted major excavations at the Athenian Agora (Camp, *The Athenian Agora*), Corinth (L. S. Meritt, *History of the American School of Classical Studies at Athens*, 151–72), Assos (Winterer, *Classicism*, 163–70), and elsewhere, produced pioneering, fundamental work on Athenian tribute lists (B. D. Meritt, *Athenian Financial Documents and Documents on Athenian Tribute*; and B. D. Meritt et al., *The Athenian*

Tribute Lists), and invested in the papyrological excavations at Oxyrhynchus and elsewhere.

91 See the debate quoted by Veysey, *Emergence*, 184.

92 Veysey, *Emergence*, 182.

93 Habinek, "Grecian Wonders and Roman Woe," 237–39, suggests some reason for the shrinking of the canon within classics itself.

Chapter 3

1 Although the number of students enrolled in Latin at all levels of American higher education increased slightly between 1980 (25,035) and 2002 (29,841), Latin enrollments as a percentage of all foreign-language enrollments fell steadily: 1980, 2.7%; 1986, 2.5%; 1990, 2.4%; 1995, 2.3%; 1998, 2.2%; 2002, 2.1%. In 1980, 22,111 undergraduate and graduate students in American colleges and universities were enrolled in ancient Greek, 2.4% of the total foreign-language enrollment. By 1986 Greek could claim only 17,608 students, 1.8% of total foreign-language enrollment. Through the 1990s Greek enrollments remained steady at about 1.4% or 1.5% of total foreign language enrollment; in 2002, there were 20,376 undergraduate and graduate students enrolled in Greek, 1.5% of total foreign-language enrollment. These figures must be seen against the background of nearly 16.5 million undergraduates in American colleges and universities. The position in secondary education seems somewhat better, leading some observers to excessively optimistic forecasts of a resurgence in Latin study; the fact is, in public secondary schools in 1990, Latin accounted for 3.7% of the enrollments in foreign languages, 163,923 students. Spanish, in contrast, had 2,611,367 students, 61.6% of foreign-language enrollment. Greek enrollments in secondary schools are almost too small to count — perhaps a few thousand students. See Brod and Huber, "Foreign Language Enrollments," and Modern Language Association of America, "Foreign Language Enrollments."

2 Said, *The World, the Text, and the Critic*, 171.

3 Most Marxist critics now reject the stricter forms of the base-superstructure model; see Rose, "The Case for Not Ignoring Marx in the Study of Women in Antiquity."

4 Hyde, "The Promise of the College," 477.

5 On Cory, see Brett, *Ionicus*, and Carter, *William Johnson Cory, 1823–1892*.

6 Gallagher, "How We Become What We Are."

7 Martin Bernal, "Classics in Crisis: An Outsider's View In," in Culham and Edmunds, *Classics*, 68.

8 Here I glide over the question of what "subjectively" might mean; for a suggestion, see Barkow, *Cosmides*, and Tooby, *The Adapted Mind*, ch. 2.

9 Kennedy, "The History of Latin Instruction."

10 Several textbooks using one or both of these methods have appeared in the past four decades: the *Cambridge Latin Course*, the *Ecce Romani* series, Hans Oerberg's *Lingua Latina Secundum Naturae Rationem* (perhaps the only successful oral-aural method), the *Oxford Latin Course*, and Jones and Sidwell's *Reading Latin*.

11 Advisory Committee of the American Classical League, *The Classical Investigation*, 32.

12 For a summary of the dispute on composition, see Pearcy, "Writing Latin in Schools and Colleges."

13 Davis, *Latin in American Schools*, 49.

14 Culham, "Decentering the Text."

15 Cicero, *Pro Caelio* 6.

16 All translations are from the Loeb edition (Hendrickson 1971).

17 *Neque solum rusticam asperitatem sed etiam peregrinam insolentiam fugere discamus* (Cic. de Or. 3.44).

18 *Ut Latine loquamur non solum videndum est ut et verba efferamus ea quae nemo iure reprehendat, et ea sic et casibus et temporibus et genere et numero conservemus ut ne quid perturbatum ac discrepans aut praeposterum sit, sed etiam lingua et spiritus et vocis sonus est ipse moderandus* (Cic. de Or. 3.40).

19 Morgan, *Literate Education in the Hellenistic and Roman Worlds*, 152–82.

20 Ibid., 185.

21 For an introduction to these prolific theorists, see Oliver, *French Feminism Reader*; Irigaray, *To Speak Is Never Neutral*; Kristeva, *Desire in Language*.

22 On this fit in the classicizing Latinity of the High Middle Ages, see Townsend and Taylor, *The Tongue of the Fathers*.

23 Diogenes Laertius 7.83 = Von Arnim, *Stoicorum Veterum Fragmenta*, 2.130 = Long and Sedley, *The Hellenistic Philosophers*, 31C.

24 Diogenes Laertius 7.43 = Long and Sedley, *Hellenistic*, 31A, 7. Stoic doctrine of grammar differs in important ways from the descriptive grammar underlying traditional instruction in classical languages; see Frede, *Essays in Ancient Philosophy*, 301–37. Even so, Stoic doctrine underlies important parts of the traditional grammar of schools; ibid., 338–59.

25 Hacking, *Why Does Language Matter to Philosophy?*, 165.

26 Freud, *The Complete Psychological Works of Sigmund Freud*, 18:14–15; a shorter version at *Interpretation of Dreams*, ibid., 5:461n.

27 Russell, *The Problems of Philosophy*, 93.

28 See for example Foucault, *Birth of a Clinic* and *Discipline and Punish*.

29 Dennett, *Consciousness Explained*; see also Damasio, *Descartes' Error*.

30 *Tractatus* 1.1.

31 The tradition is dead; our task is to revivify life that has passed away. We know that ghosts cannot speak until they have drunk blood; and the spirits which we evoke demand the blood of our hearts. We give it to them gladly; but if they then abide our question, something from us has entered into them; something alien, that must be cast out, cast out in the name of truth! (Quoted above, p. 38.)

32 Dennett, *Consciousness Explained*, 139–40.

33 Wilamowitz, *Erinnerungen* and *My Recollections*.

34 I encourage people to test this idea by reading Wilamowitz's account of the trial and death of Socrates (Wilamowitz, *Platon*, 155–79) and the preface to Vlastos, *Socrates, Ironist and Moral Philosopher*. See also Calder, "Ecce Homo."

35 This criterion of meaning, verifiability, was articulated in the 1920s by Karl-Gottlob Frege and other philosophers of the Vienna Circle. Philosophers of science, beginning with Karl Popper, ceased to regard verifiability as an adequate criterion for the universal statements of science — yet another confirmation that *Altertumswissenschaft* is not science. Hacking, *Why Does Language Matter?*, 95; Ayer, *Language, Truth, and Logic*; Popper, *The Logic of Scientific Discovery*.

36 Pauly, Wissowa, and Kroll, *Realencyclopädie*.

37 Cancik and Schneider, *Der Neue Pauly*.

38 Arrowsmith, "Nietzsche," 296–97. Emphases in original.

39 Ibid., 291. Emphases in original.

40 See in particular *Metaphysics* 3, especially 1, 995a–996a.

41 *The Idea of a University*, Discourse V (Ker, *Newman*, 102).

42 Damasio, *Descartes' Error*.

43 Dennett, *Consciousness Explained*.

44 Feynman, *What Do You Care What Other People Think?*, 244.

45 Searle, *Minds, Brains, and Science*; Penrose, *The Emperor's New Mind*; Dennett, Review of *The Emperor's New Mind* and *Consciousness Explained*.

46 Dewey, *Intelligence in the Modern World*, 317.

47 Ker, *Newman*, 154.

Chapter 4

1   As I write this, *Troy*, a film loosely based on the *Iliad*, is playing in theaters, another on Alexander the Great is in production, and one on Hannibal is being contemplated.

2   Among predecessors, consider for example John Jay Chapman and William Arrowsmith; for both, see *Arion* 3rd series 2.2 and 2.3 (1992/1993), a special issue in memory of Arrowsmith.

3   In what follows, my debt to Boeckh, *Enzyklopaedie*, and to Gadamer, *Truth and Method*, will, I hope, be evident even where I have not cited specific pages.

4   My examples come from latest issue of *The Journal of Hellenic Studies*; Burnyeat, "*Apology* 304b 2–4"; Gainsford, "Formal Analysis of Recognition Scenes in the *Odyssey*"; and Kovacs, "Toward a Reconstruction of *Iphigenia Aulidensis*."

5   Gadamer, *Truth and Method*, 171–218.

6   Ibid., 399.

7   The debate over "authentic performance" of medieval and Renaissance music provides a paradigmatic illustration of the issues raised by presentation of works from a past so distant that it has become alien; see Taruskin, *Text and Act*; Butt, *Playing with History*.

8   On the relation between readers' experience and allusion, see Hinds, *Allusion and Intertext*, and especially Edmunds, *Intertextuality and the Reading of Roman Poetry*.

9   Thomas, *Virgil and the Augustan Reception*, xi.

10 Gadamer, *Truth and Method*, 362–79.

11 Buber, "Between Man and Man," 114.

12 Not a question chosen at random; see Adkin, "Did the Romans Keep Their Underwear on in Bed?," followed by Olson, "Roman Underwear Revisited."

13 This passage through "young adulthood" is ably documented by Parks, *Big Questions, Worthy Dreams*.

14 Jardine, Clifford, and Friesen, *Back to the Basics of Teaching and Learning*.

15 Ibid., 3.

16 Wilamowitz, *Geschichte der Philologie* and *History of Classical Scholarship*.

17 Calder and Kramer, *Introductory Bibliography*, documents the growth.

18 E.g. Too and Livingstone, *Pedagogy and Power*; Stray, *Classics Transformed* and *Classics in 19th- and 20th-Century Cambridge*.

19 E.g. Thomas, *Virgil*; Winterer, *Culture*.

20 Bernard Knox in Fagles, *The Iliad of Homer*, 12.

21 Hanson and Heath, "The Good," 39.

22 Putnam, *Pragmatism*.

23 The case is argued in Pinker, *The Blank State*.

24 From an enormous literature see Benacerraf and Putnam, *Philosophy of Mathematics* and Benacerraf, "Mathematical Truth."

25 Roger Scruton's example: Scruton, *An Intelligent Person's Guide to Philosophy*, 41.

26 For these understandings of the self, see Trilling, *Sincerity and Authenticity*.

27 This understanding of the ancient self is essentially that of Gill, *Personality in Greek Epic, Tragedy, and Philosophy*; see also for example Williams, *Shame and Necessity* and MacIntyre, *After Virtue*. I use "indeterminate" and "negotiable" for what Gill calls an "objective-participant" conception of the self.

28 Gill, *Personality*, 6–8 and 400–69.

29 Wittgenstein's "private language" argument, on which see Scruton, *Modern Philosophy*, 46–57.

30 Gill, *Personality*, 2.

31 This idea that we know the Greeks and Romans because we come to them with "foreknowledge" derives from Heidegger; see Gadamer, *Truth and Method*, 265–71. Ancient mathematical thought provides a useful contrasting example; in this case, because mathematics (Euclid excepted) is not part of our common picture of the ancient world, as character or personality is, an ancient mathematician's way of thinking can seem profoundly alien; see Netz, *The Works of Archimedes*, and Dickey, Review of Netz.

32 For an introduction to the topic of medical sects, see Scarborough, *Roman Medicine*, 38–51.

33 *Eudemian Ethics* I.5 1216b 22–25. On the analogy between medicine and philosophical ethics, see Nussbaum, *The Therapy of Desire*.

34 Macintyre, *After Virtue*, 146–64.

35 Nussbaum, *Desire*, 488.

36 *Iliad* 19.85–89, tr. Lattimore.

37 Taplin, "Agamemnon's Role in the *Iliad*," 62.

38 On Agamemnon's apology see Taplin, "Agamemnon's Role," and Dodds, *The Greeks and the Irrational*, 1–27.

39 E.g. Vergil, *Aeneid* 2.567–87.

40 *Iliad* 3.164.

41 *Iliad* 3.410–12.

42 *Iliad* 12.311–28.

43 Most recently Proctor, *Defining the Humanities*.

44 "To the Reader," Montaigne, *The Complete Essays of Montaigne*, 2.

45 Quoted in Zeitlin, *The Essays of Michel de Montaigne*, xxxiv.

46 "Of Education," Montaigne, *Complete Essays*, 107.

47 Ibid., 111.

48 Plutarch, *Crassus* 2.2.

49 Matthew 20:2; a legionary received about two-thirds of a denarius per day.

50 Iraq and Afghanistan, as of August 2003.

51 See also *Classical World* 97.1 (2003), a special issue on applying the ancient world to the events of September 11, 2001.

52 For a readable polemic against this kind of misrepresentation of ancient Greek society, see duBois, *Trojan Horses*.

53 "After all, establishing the fixed text has been the humanistic raison d'être since the Renaissance. To nail it down forever and then finally explain it, that has been what literary scholars do. All our tunes of glory vary this central theme, even our current endeavors to show once and for all why nobody can once and for all explain anything" (Lanham, *Electronic Word*, 7).

WORKS CITED

Adkin, Neil. "Did the Romans Keep Their Underwear on in Bed?" *Classical World* 93 (2000): 619–20.

Advisory Committee of the American Classical League. *The Classical Investigation, Part One, The General Report*. Princeton: Princeton University Press, 1924.

Arrowsmith, William. "Nietzsche: Notes for 'We Philologists,'" *Arion* n.s. 1, no. 2 (1973/74): 279–380.

Ayer, A. J. *Language, Truth, and Logic*. London: Victor Gollancz, 1936.

Baker, J. E. "The Victorian Chronology of Our Liberal Education," *Journal of Higher Education* 18 (1947): 414–16.

Balfour, Ian. *The Rhetoric of Romantic Prophecy*. Stanford: Stanford University Press, 2002.

Baring-Gould, William S., ed. *The Annotated Sherlock Holmes*. 2 vols. New York: Potter, 1967.

Barkow, James, Leda Cosmides, and John Tooby, eds. *The Adapted Mind: Evolutionary Psychology and the Generation of Culture*. New York: Oxford University Press, 1992.

Benacerraf, Paul. "Mathematical Truth," *Journal of Philosophy* 70 (1973): 661–79.

Benacerraf, Paul, and Hilary Putnam. *Philosophy of Mathematics*. Englewood Cliffs: Prentice- Hall, 1964.

Bentinck-Smith, William, ed. *The Harvard Book: Selections from Three Centuries.* Cambridge, Mass.: Harvard University Press, 1982.

Bietenholz, Peter G. *Historia and Fabula: Myths and Legends in Historical Thought from Antiquity to the Modern Age.* Leiden: Brill, 1994.

Bloom, Allan. *The Closing of the American Mind.* New York: Simon & Schuster, 1987.

Boeckh, August. *Enzyklopaedie und Methodologie der philologischen Wissenschaften.* Edited by Ernst Bratuscheck. Leipzig: Teubner, 1886.

(Brett) Reginald, Viscount Esher. *Ionicus.* Garden City: Doubleday, Page, 1924.

Brian, Denis. *Einstein, A Life.* New York: Wiley, 1996.

Briggs, Ward W. Jr., ed. *Biographical Dictionary of North American Classicists.* Westport, Conn.: Greenwood Press and American Philological Association, 1994.

— — —. *The Letters of Basil Lanneau Gildersleeve.* Baltimore: Johns Hopkins University Press, 1987.

Brod, Richard, and Betinna J. Huber. "Foreign Language Enrollments in U.S. Institutions of Higher Education, Fall, 1990," *ADFL Bulletin* 23, no. 3 (1990): 7–10.

Broughton, T. R. S. *Magistrates of the Roman Republic.* New York: American Philological Association, 1951.

Buber, Martin. *Between Man and Man.* London: Routledge & Kegan Paul, 1947; repr. Routledge 2002.

Burnyeat, Miles. "*Apology* 304b 2–4: Socrates, Money, and the Grammar of γίγνεσθαι," *Journal of Hellenic Studies* 123 (2003): 1–25.

Bursian, Conrad. *Geschichte der classischen Philologie in Deutschland.* 2 vols. Munich: Oldenbourg, 1883.

Bushnell, Rebecca. *A Culture of Teaching.* Ithaca: Cornell University Press, 1996.

Butt, John. *Playing with History: The Historical Approach to Musical Performance.* Cambridge: Cambridge University Press, 2002.

Butterfield, L. H., ed. *Letters of Benjamin Rush.* Memoirs of the American Philosophical Society 30, pts. 1 and 2. Princeton: American Philosophical Society, 1951.

Calder, William M. III. "Classical Scholarship in the United States: An Introductory Essay." In *Biographical Dictionary of North American Classicists,* by Ward W. Briggs, Jr., xix–xxxix. Westport, Conn.: Greenwood Press and American Philological Association, 1994.

———. "Ecce Homo: The Autobiographical in Wilamowitz's Scholarly Writings." In *Wilamowitz nach 50 Jahren*, 80-110. Darmstadt: Wissenschaftliche Buchgesellschaft, 1985.

———. "The Refugee Classical Scholars in the USA: An Evaluation of their Contribution," *Illinois Classical Studies* 17 (1992): 153–73.

———. *Werner Jaeger Reconsidered*. Illinois Classical Studies, suppl. 3. Atlanta: Scholars Press, 1990.

———. "The Wilamowitz-Nietzsche Struggle: New Documents and a Reappraisal," *Nietzsche-Studien* 12 (1983): 214–54.

Calder, William M. III, and D. J. Kramer. *An Introductory Bibliography to the History of Classical Scholarship, Chiefly in the XIXth and XXth Centuries.* Hildesheim: Georg Olms, 1992.

Camp, John M. *The Athenian Agora: Excavations in the Heart of Classical Athens.* London: Thames & Hudson, 1986.

Cancik, Hubert, and Helmut Schneider, eds. *Der Neue Pauly: Enzyklopädie der Antike.* 10 vols. Stuttgart: Metzler, 1996–2004.

Cappon, Lester J., ed. *The Adams-Jefferson Letters.* 2 vols. Chapel Hill: University of North Carolina Press, 1959.

Carter, John. *William Johnson Cory, 1823–1892.* Cambridge: Rampant Lions Press, 1959.

Clark, Harry Hayden, ed. *Thomas Paine: Representative Selections, with Introduction, Bibliography, and Notes.* New York: American Book, 1944.

Clarke, Martin L. *Classical Education in Britain 1500–1900.* Cambridge: Cambridge University Press, 1959.

Conkin, Paul. *Puritans and Pragmatists: Eight Eminent American Thinkers.* New York: Dodd, Mead, 1968.

Conway, Moncure D., ed. *The Writings of Thomas Paine.* 4 vols. New York: Putnam, 1894–1896.

Cremin, Lawrence A. *American Education: The Colonial Experience 1607–1783.* New York: Harper & Row, 1970.

Culham, Phyllis. "Decentering the Text: The Case of Ovid," *Helios* 17, no. 2 (1990): 161–70.

Culham, Phyllis, Lowell and Edmunds, eds. *Classics: A Discipline and Profession in Crisis?* Lanham, Md.: University Press of America, 1989.

Damasio, Antonio. *Descartes' Error: Emotion, Reason, and the Human Brain.* New York: Putnam, 1994.

Darwin, Charles, and Thomas Henry Huxley. *Autobiographies.* Edited by Gavin de Beer. London: Oxford University Press, 1974.

Davis, Sally. *Latin in American Schools: Teaching the Ancient World.* Atlanta: Scholars Press, 1991.

Dennett, Daniel C. *Consciousness Explained.* Boston: Little, Brown, 1991.

— — —. *Darwin's Dangerous Idea: Evolution and the Meanings of Life.* New York: Simon & Schuster, 1995.

— — —. Review of *The Emperor's New Mind,* by Roger Penrose. *Times Literary Supplement,* September 29–October 5, 1989.

Dewey, John. *Intelligence in the Modern World.* Edited by Joseph Ratner. New York: Random House, 1929.

Dickey, Eleanor. Review of *The Works of Archimedes,* by Reviel Netz. *Bryn Mawr Classical Review* 2004.07.14. http://ccat.sas.upenn.edu/bmcr/2004/2004-07-14.html. Accessed July 31, 2004.

Diehl, Carl. *Americans and German Scholarship 1770–1870.* New Haven: Yale University Press, 1978.

Dodds, Eric Robertson. *The Greeks and the Irrational.* Berkeley: University of California Press, 1951.

duBois, Page. *Trojan Horses: Saving the Classics from Conservatives.* New York: New York University Press, 2001.

Edmunds, Lowell. *Intertextuality and the Reading of Roman Poetry.* Baltimore: Johns Hopkins University Press, 2001.

Emberly, Peter C., and Walter R. Newell. *Bankrupt Education: The Decline of Liberal Education in Canada.* Toronto: University of Toronto Press, 1994.

Emerson, Ralph Waldo. *The Collected Works of Ralph Waldo Emerson.* Vol. 1, *Nature, Addresses, and Lectures.* Edited by Robert E. Spiller and Alfred R. Ferguson. Cambridge, Mass.: Harvard University Press, 1971.

— — —. *Nature. Addresses and Lectures.* Edited by Edward W. Emerson. Boston: Houghton Mifflin, 1903.

Fagles, Robert, trans. *The Iliad of Homer.* New York: Viking, 1990.

Fallows, James. "When George Meets John," *Atlantic,* July–August 2004, 67–80.

Feynman, Richard. *"What Do You Care What Other People Think?"* New York: Bantam, 1988.

Ford, Susan. "Thomas Jefferson and John Adams on the Classics," *Arion* 6 (1967): 116–32.

Foucault, Michel. *Birth of the Clinic.* New York: Pantheon Books, 1973.

— — —. *Discipline and Punish.* New York: Pantheon Books, 1977.

Fraenkel, Eduard. "Review of *Servianorum Commentariorum Editionis Harvardianae* Volumen II," *Journal of Roman Studies* 38 (1948): 131–43 =

Kleine Beiträge zur Klassischen Philologie (Rome: Edizioni di storia e letteratura, 1964), 339–90.

Franklin, Benjamin. *Benjamin Franklin: Writings*. Edited by J. A. Leo Lemay. Literary Classics of the United States. New York: Library of America, 1987.

Frede, Michael. *Essays in Ancient Philosophy*. Minneapolis: University of Minnesota Press, 1987.

Freud, Sigmund. *The Standard Edition of the Complete Psychological Works of Sigmund Freud*. Edited and translated by James Strachey, 21 vols. London: Hogarth Press, 1953–1974.

Gadamer, Hans-Georg. *Truth and Method*. Translated by Joel Weinsheimer and Donald G. Marshall, 2nd ed. New York: Continuum International Publishing Group, 1989.

Gainsford, Peter. "Formal Analysis of Recognition Scenes in the *Odyssey*," *Journal of Hellenic Studies* 123 (2003): 41–59.

Galinsky, G. Karl. "The *Aeneid* as a Guide to Life," *Augustan Age* 7 (1987): 161–73.

———, ed. *The Interpretation of Roman Poetry: Empiricism or Hermeneutics?* Studien zur klassischen Philologie 67. Frankfurt am Main: Peter Lang, 1992.

Gallagher, Winifred. "How We Become What We Are," *Atlantic Monthly*, September 1994, 38–55.

Gay, Peter. *The Enlightenment: An Interpretation*. New York: Knopf, 1967.

Gildersleeve, Basil L. "The Agamemnon at Oxford," *Nation*, June 24, 1880, 472.

Gill, Christopher. *Personality in Greek Epic, Tragedy, and Philosophy*. Oxford: Clarendon Press, 1996.

Giraud, Jean. "Victorin de Feltre (1378–1447?)" *Paedagogica Historica* 11 (1971): 369–87.

Graff, Gerald. *Professing Literature: An Institutional History*. Chicago: University of Chicago Press, 1987.

Grafton, Anthony. *Joseph Scaliger: A Study in the History of Classical Scholarship*. Oxford: Clarendon Press, 1983.

Grafton, Anthony, Glenn W. Most, and James E. G. Zetzel, eds. *F. A. Wolf, Prolegomena to Homer*. Princeton: Princeton University Press, 1985.

Grafton, Anthony, and Lisa Jardine. *From Humanism to the Humanities: Education and the Liberal Arts in Fifteenth- and Sixteenth-Century Europe*. Cambridge, Mass.: Harvard University Press, 1986.

Green, Peter. "Mandarins and Iconoclasts," *Arion* 6, no. 3 (1999): 122–49.

Green, V. H. H. *A History of Oxford University*. London: Batsford, 1974.

Grummond, Nancy Thomson, de. *An Encyclopedia of the History of Classical Archaeology*. Westport, Conn.: Greenwood Press, 1996.

Gutmann, Amy. *Democratic Education*. Princeton: Princeton University Press, 1987.

Habinek, Thomas. "Grecian Wonders and Roman Woe: the Romantic Rejection of Rome and its Consequences for the Study of Roman Literature." In *The Interpretation of Roman Poetry: Empiricism or Hermeneutics?*, edited by Karl G. Galinsky, 227–42. Frankfurt am Main: Peter Lang, 1992.

Hacking, Ian. *Why Does Language Matter to Philosophy?* Cambridge: Cambridge University Press, 1995.

Hallett, Judith P. "Writing as an American in Classical Scholarship." In *Compromising Traditions: The Personal Voice in Classical Scholarship*, edited by Judith P. Hallett and Thomas Van Nortwick, 120-152. London: Routledge, 1996.

Hanson, Victor Davis, and John Heath. "The Good, the Bad, and the Ugly," *Arion* 6, no. 3 (1999): 150–95.

— — —. *Who Killed Homer? The Demise of Classical Education and the Recovery of Greek Wisdom*. New York: Free Press, 1998.

Heath, John. "More Quarreling in the Muses' Birdcage," *Arion* 6, no. 2 (1998): 141–79.

Hendrickson, G. L., and H. M. Hubbell, trans. *Brutus*, by Cicero. Cambridge, Mass.: Harvard University Press, 1971.

Henrichs, Albert. "The Last of the Detractors: Friedrich Nietzsche's Condemnation of Euripides," *Greek Roman and Byzantine Studies* 27 (1986): 369–97.

Hinds, Stephen. *Allusion and Intertext: Dynamics of Appropriation in Roman Poetry*. Cambridge: Cambridge University Press, 1998.

Hirsch, E. D. *Validity in Interpretation*. New Haven: Yale University Press, 1967.

Hofstadter, Richard, and Wilson Smith, eds. *American Higher Education: A Documentary History*. Chicago: University of Chicago Press, 1961.

Honeywell, Roy. *The Educational Work of Thomas Jefferson*. Cambridge, Mass.: Harvard University Press, 1931.

Horowitz, Helen Lefkowitz. *The Power and Passion of M. Carey Thomas*. New York: Knopf, 1994.

Hyde, William DeWitt. "The Promise of the College," *Educational Review* 28 (1904): 461–77.

Irigaray, Luce. *To Speak Is Never Neutral*. Translated by Gail Schwab. New York: Routledge, 2002.

Jaeger, Werner. *Scripta Minora*, 2 vols. Rome: Edizioni di storia e letteratura, 1960.

Jardine, David W., Patricia Clifford, and Sharon Friesen. *Back to the Basics of Teaching and Learning: Thinking the World Together*. Mahwah, NJ: Lawrence Erlbaum, 2003.

Kallendorf, Craig W., ed. and trans. *Humanist Educational Treatises*. The I Tatti Renaissance Library 5. Cambridge, Mass.: Harvard University Press, 2002.

Kennedy, George A. "The History of Latin Instruction," *Helios* 14, no. 2 (1987): 7–16.

Kenney, E. J. *The Classical Text: Aspects of Editing in the Age of the Printed Book*. Berkeley: University of California Press, 1974.

Ker, I. T., ed. *John Henry Newman: The Idea of a University Defined and Illustrated*. Oxford: Clarendon Press, 1976.

Kimball, Bruce A. *Orators and Philosophers: A History of the Idea of Liberal Education*. New York: Teachers College, Columbia University, 1986.

Kimmerle, Heinz, trans. *F. D. E. Schleiermacher, Hermeneutics: The Handwritten Manuscripts*. Missoula, Mont.: Scholars Press for the American Academy of Religion, 1977.

Kovacs, David. "Toward a Reconstruction of *Iphigenia Aulidensis*," *Journal of Hellenic Studies* 123 (2003): 77–103.

Kristeva, Julia. *Desire in Language: A Semiotic Approach to Literature and Art*. Edited by Leon S. Roudiez, et al. New York: Columbia University Press, 1980.

Lanham, Richard A. *The Electronic Word: Democracy, Technology, and the Arts*. Chicago: The University of Chicago Press, 1993.

Lloyd-Jones, Hugh. *Blood for the Ghosts*. Baltimore: Johns Hopkins University Press, 1982.

Locke, John. *Some Thoughts Concerning Education*. Edited by John W. and Jean S. Yoltin. Oxford: Clarendon Press, 1987.

Long, A. A., and D. N. Sedley. *The Hellenistic Philosophers*. 2 vols. Cambridge: Cambridge University Press, 1987.

Long, Orie William. *Literary Pioneers: Early American Explorers of European Culture*. Cambridge, Mass.: Harvard University Press, 1935.

MacIntyre, Alasdair. *After Virtue: A Study in Moral Theory.* 2nd ed. Notre Dame: University of Notre Dame Press, 1984.

Mansfeld, Jaap. "The Wilamowitz-Nietzsche Struggle: Another New Document and Some Further Comments," *Nietzsche-Studien* 15 (1986): 41–58.

Marchand, Suzanne L. *Down from Olympus: Archaeology and Philhellenism in Germany, 1750–1970.* Princeton: Princeton University Press, 1996.

Marsden, George W. *The Soul of the American University: From Protestant Establishment to Established Nonbelief.* New York: Oxford University Press, 1994.

McInerny, Ralph. "Beyond the Liberal Arts." In *The Seven Liberal Arts in the Middle Ages,* edited by David L.Wagner, 248-272. Bloomington: Indiana University Press, 1983.

Meritt, Benjamin D. *Athenian Financial Documents of the Fifth Century.* Ann Arbor: University of Michigan Press, 1932.

— — —. *Documents on Athenian Tribute.* Cambridge, Mass.: Harvard University Press, 1937.

Meritt, Benjamin D., H. T. Wade-Gery, and Malcolm Francis McGregor. *The Athenian Tribute Lists.* 4 vols. Cambridge, Mass.: Harvard University Press, 1939–1953.

Meritt, Lucy S. *History of the American School of Classical Studies at Athens, 1939–1980.* Princeton: American School of Classical Studies at Athens, 1984.

Montaigne, Michel Eyquem de. *The Complete Essays of Montaigne.* Translated by Donald M. Frame. Stanford: Stanford University Press, 1965.

Morgan, Teresa. *Literate Education in the Hellenistic and Roman Worlds.* New York: Cambridge University Press, 1998.

Morris, Jan, ed. *The Oxford Book of Oxford.* Oxford: Oxford University Press, 1978.

Most, Glenn W. "One Hundred Years of Fractiousness: Disciplining Polemics in Nineteenth-Century German Classical Scholarship," *Transactions of the American Philological Association* 127 (1997): 349–61.

Netz, Reviel, ed. and trans. *The Works of Archimedes: Translated into English, Together with Eutocius' Commentaries, with Commentary, and Critical Edition of the Diagrams.* Vol. 1, *The Two Books on the Sphere and the Cylinder.* Cambridge: Cambridge University Press, 2004.

Nietzsche, Friedrich. *The Birth of Tragedy and The Case of Wagner.* Translated by Walter Kaufmann. New York: Random House, 1967.

Nussbaum, Martha. *The Therapy of Desire: Theory and Practice in Hellenistic Ethics.* Princeton: Princeton University Press, 1994.

Oliver, Kelly, ed. *French Feminism Reader.* Lanham, Md.: Rowman & Littlefield, 2000.

Olson, Kelly. "Roman Underwear Revisited." *Classical World* 96 (2003): 201–10.

Ong, Walter J. "Latin Language Study as a Renaissance Puberty Rite," *Studies in Philology* 56, no. 2 (1959): 103–24.

Paglia, Camille. "Junk Bonds and Corporate Raiders: Academe in the Hour of the Wolf," *Arion* 3rd ser. 1, no. 2 (1991): 139–212.

Pangle, Lorraine Smith, and Thomas L. Pangle. *The Learning of Liberty: The Educational Ideas of the American Founders.* Lawrence: University Press of Kansas, 1993.

Parks, Sharon. *Big Questions, Worthy Dreams: Mentoring Young Adults in their Search for Meaning, Purpose, and Faith.* San Francisco: Jossey-Bass, 2000.

Pattison, Robert. *The Great Dissent: John Henry Newman and the Liberal Heresy.* New York: Oxford University Press, 1991.

Pauly, August Friedrich von, G. Wissowa, and W. Kroll. *Realencyclopädie der Classischen Altertumswissenschaft.* Stuttgart: Metzler, 1893–1972.

Pearcy, Lee T. "Aristophanes in Philadelphia: The *Acharnians* of 1886," *Classical World* 96 (2003): 299–313.

———. "Writing Latin in Schools and Colleges," *Classical World* 92 (1998): 35–42.

Pease, Arthur Stanley, ed. *Publi Vergili Maronis Aeneidos Liber Quartus.* Cambridge, Mass.: Harvard University Press, 1935.

Pelling, Christopher, ed. *Characterization and Individuality in Greek Literature.* Oxford: Clarendon Press, 1990.

Penrose, Roger. *The Emperor's New Mind: Concerning Computers, Minds, and the Laws of Physics.* New York: Oxford University Press, 1989.

Pfeiffer, Rudolf. *History of Classical Scholarship from the Beginnings to the End of the Hellenistic Age.* Oxford: Oxford University Press, 1968.

———. *History of Classical Scholarship from 1300 to 1850.* Oxford: Oxford University Press, 1976.

Pinker, Steven. *The Blank Slate: The Modern Denial of Human Nature.* New York: Viking, 2002.

Popper, Karl. *The Logic of Scientific Discovery.* New York: Harper & Row, 1968.

Potts, Alex. *Flesh and the Ideal: Winckelmann and the Origins of Art History.* New Haven: Yale University Press, 1994.

Pritchard, J. P., ed. and trans. *On Interpretation and Criticism,* by August Boeckh. Norman: University of Oklahoma Press, 1968.

Proctor, Robert E. *Defining the Humanities: How Rediscovering a Tradition Can Improve our Schools.* Bloomington: Indiana University Press, 1998.

Putnam, Hilary. *Pragmatism: An Open Question.* Cambridge, Mass.: Blackwell, 1995.

Rabinowitz, Nancy Sorkin, and Amy Richlin, eds. *Feminist Theory and the Classics.* New York: Routledge, 1993.

Rand, E. K., et al. *Servianorum in Vergilii Carmina Commentariorum Editionis Harvardianae,* volumen II. Lancaster, Pa.: American Philological Association, 1946.

Reinhold, Meyer. *Classica Americana: The Greek and Roman Heritage in the United States.* Detroit: Wayne State University Press, 1984.

Remini, Robert V. *Andrew Jackson and the Course of American Democracy, 1833–1845.* New York: Harper & Row, 1984.

Richardson, Robert D. *Emerson: The Mind on Fire.* Berkeley: University of California Press, 1995.

Rose, Peter W. "The Case for Not Ignoring Marx in the Study of Women in Antiquity." In *Feminist Theory and the Classics,* edited by Nancy Rabinowitz and Amy Richlin, 211–37. New York: Routledge 1993.

Rothblatt, Sheldon. *The Modern University and its Discontents: The Fate of Newman's Legacies in Britain and America.* Cambridge: Cambridge University Press, 1997.

Ruegg, Walter. "The University: Product and Shaper of Society." In *History of the University in Europe.* Vol. 1, *Universities in the Middle Ages,* edited by Hilde de Ridder-Symoens, 9-14. Cambridge: Cambridge University Press, 1992.

Russell, Bertrand. *The Problems of Philosophy.* New York: Henry Holt, 1912.

Said, Edward W. *The World, the Text, and the Critic.* Cambridge, Mass.: Harvard University Press, Cambridge, 1983.

Santayana, George. *Character and Opinion in the United States with Reminiscences of William James and Josiah Royce and Academic Life in America.* London: Scribner, 1920.

Scarborough, John. *Roman Medicine.* London: Thames & Hudson, 1969.

Schelling, F. W. J. *On University Studies.* Edited by N. Guterman. Translated by E. S. Morgan. Athens: Ohio University Press, 1966.

Schröder, Eduard. "Philologiae studiosus," *Neue Jahrbücher für das klassische Altertum* 32 (1913): 168–71.

Scruton, Roger. *An Intelligent Person's Guide to Philosophy*. New York: Penguin Books, 1998.

— — —. *Modern Philosophy: An Introduction and Survey*. New York: Penguin Books, 1994.

Searle, John. *Minds, Brains, and Science*. Cambridge, Mass.: Harvard University Press, 1984.

Simpson, David, ed. *German Aesthetic and Literary Criticism: Kant, Fichte, Schelling, Schopenhauer, Hegel*. New York: Cambridge University Press, 1984.

Stray, Christopher. *Classics Transformed: Schools, Universities, and Society in England, 1830–1960*. Oxford: Clarendon Press, 1998.

— — —, ed. *Classics in 19th- and 20th-Century Cambridge: Curriculum, Culture, and Community*. Cambridge: Cambridge Philological Society, 1999.

Taplin, Oliver. "Agamemnon's Role in the *Iliad*." In *Characterization and Individuality in Greek Literature*, edited by Christopher Pelling, 60–82. Oxford: Clarendon Press, 1990.

Taruskin, Richard. *Text and Act: Essays on Music and Performance*. New York: Oxford University Press, 1995.

Thomas, Richard F. *Virgil and the Augustan Reception*. Cambridge: Cambridge University Press, 2001.

Tocqueville, Alexis de. *Democracy in America*. Edited by Phillips Bradley. New York: Knopf, 1945.

Too, Yun Lee, and Niall Livingstone. *Pedagogy and Power: Rhetorics of Classical Learning*. Cambridge: Cambridge University Press, 1998.

Townsend, David, and Andrew Taylor, eds. *The Tongue of the Fathers: Gender and Ideology in Twelfth-Century Latin*. Philadelphia: University of Pennsylvania Press, 1998.

Trilling, Lionel. *Sincerity and Authenticity*. Cambridge, Mass: Harvard University Press, 1972.

Van Sickle, John. "Towards Interculturalism in Class," *Classical World* 91 (1997): 47–52.

Veysey, Laurence R. *The Emergence of the American University*. Chicago: University of Chicago Press, 1965.

Vlastos, Gregory. *Socrates, Ironist and Moral Philosopher*. Ithaca: Cornell University Press, 1991.

Von Arnim, H. *Stoicorum Veterum Fragmenta*. Leipzig: Teubner, 1964.

White, Donald O. "Werner Jaeger's 'Third Humanism' and the Crisis of Conservative Cultural Politics in Weimar Germany." In *Werner Jaeger Reconsidered* by William M. Calder III, 267–88. Atlanta: Scholars Press, 1990.

Wilamowitz-Moellendorff, Ulrich von. *Einleitung in die griechische Tragödie: Euripides, Herakles*, vol. 1. Darmstadt: Wissenschaftliche Buchgesellschaft, 1889; repr. 1969.

— — —. *Erinnerungen 1848–1914*. Leipzig: Koehler, n.d.

— — —. "Future Philology! A Reply to Friedrich Nietzsche's The Birth of Tragedy." Translated by Gertrude Postl. *New Nietzsche Studies* 4 (2000): 1–32.

— — —. *Geschichte der Philologie*. Leipzig: Teubner, 1959.

— — —. *History of Classical Scholarship*. Edited and translated by Hugh Lloyd-Jones. Baltimore: Johns Hopkins University Press, 1982.

— — —. *My Recollections*. Translated by G. C. Richards. London: Chatto & Windus, 1930.

— — —. *Platon*. Berlin: Weidmannsche Buchhandlung, 1920.

Williams, Bernard. *Shame and Necessity*. Berkeley: University of California Press, 1993.

Wills, Gary. *Lincoln at Gettysburg*. New York: Simon & Schuster, 1992.

Winterer, Caroline. *The Culture of Classicism: Ancient Greece and Rome in American Intellectual Life, 1780–1910*. Baltimore: Johns Hopkins University Press, 2002.

Woodward, William H. *Vittorino da Feltre and Other Humanist Educators: Essays and Versions*. Cambridge: Cambridge University Press, 1897.

Woody, Thomas. *Early Quaker Education in Pennsylvania*. New York: Teachers College, Columbia University, 1920.

Woody, Thomas, ed. *Educational Views of Benjamin Franklin*. New York: McGraw-Hill, 1931.

Zeitlin, Jacob, trans. *The Essays of Michel de Montaigne*. New York: Knopf, 1934.

INDEX

Academia Virginiensis et Oxoniensis, 45

Academy and College of Philadelphia, 54

Acharnians (Aristophanes), in Philadelphia, 77, 78

Achilles, 137

Adam (first man), 104

Adams, John: as student of Classics, 53; *Defence of the Constitutions of the United States*, 53; 73

Aeneas, 104, 118

Aeneid (Vergil): tradition of reading, 122; student's encounter with, 128

Agamemnon (Aeschylus): at Oxford, 79; in New York, 121

Agamemnon, in the *Iliad*, 137, 138

Alaric, 142

Alexandria, 18

Altertumswissenschaft, 6, 15–22;

defined, 17; Matthew Arnold on, 17; 21; false paradigm of, 28–29, 40; Emerson's knowledge of, 60; in German universities, 75; 87, 100; end of, 106–11; as creative activity, 108; as game, 109–10; 120; American forms of, 121; Nietzsche's views on, 133; 144

American Classical League, 93

American Journal of Philology, 41

American Philological Association, 78

"American Scholar" (Emerson), 58–60

Amherst College, 61, 73

Analectic Magazine, 56

Andover (school), 8

Aphrodite, in the *Iliad*, 137–38

Appian, in Montaigne, 140

a priori ideas, 102

Michigan, University of: as
  "Catholicoepistemiad," 64; 70, 73
Middlebury College, 61
Milton, John, 49
Mitchell, Jonathan, 45
modernism: idea of self in, 134
Montaigne, Michel Yquem de,
  139–40
Morgan, Teresa, 98
Mozart, Wolfgang Amadeus: Don
  Giovanni, 107, 108
multiple intelligences, 68
Müller, Karl Otfried, 20–21
Munich, University of, 77

Nature: in Emerson's "American
  Scholar," 59
nature, human. See human nature.
neo-Hellenists, 18
Newman, John Henry, 11–15; Idea
  of a University, 12, 13, 14, 25;
  "Christianity and Letters," 13,
  112; as humanist philologue, 21;
  22; seventh Discourse on the Idea
  of a University, 24, 91; on ideal
  education in society, 24; on
  instruction in Latin and Greek,
  25; on liberal arts education, 26;
  44, 66, 69, 87, 88, 105, 113, 115
New Testament, 36
Newton, Isaac, 107–8
Nietzsche, Friedrich, 19; dispute
  with Wilamowitz, 29–41; at
  Pforte, 31; early career, 31; Birth

of Tragedy, 32, 38; views on
  Greek drama, 34; Untimely
  Meditations, 35; on Greeks as
  moral example, 36; "We
  Philologists," 36, 38; rejects
  Boeckh's unity of antiquity, 38;
  105; on philology, 110; Beyond
  Good and Evil, 111; 124, 133
nihilism, 133
Norddeutsche Allgemeine Zeitung, 33
Nussbaum, Martha, 136

objectivity: Nietzsche on, 111; 106,
  119
Odyssey (Homer), 120
Old College: defined, 61–62; in rela-
  tion to University of Virginia,
  63–64; 65, 70, 72, 74;
fossilized curriculum of, 76; in 1880s,
  78; 81
"Old Deluder Satan" act. See
  Massachusetts School Act of
  1647.
Oldfather, William Abbott, 77
Oriel College (Oxford), 11
Ovid: Metamorphoses translated by
  Sandys, 53; 95
Oxford University, 8, 16; as pattern
  for American colonial institutions,
  45; 77

Paedeia (Werner Jaeger), 80
Paine, Thomas, 52
Palmer, Edward, 45